SPECTRUM®

Reading

Kindergarten

Published by Spectrum®
an imprint of Carson-Dellosa Publishing LLC
Greensboro, NC

Spectrum®
An imprint of Carson-Dellosa Publishing LLC
P.O. Box 35665
Greensboro, NC 27425 USA

ISBN 978-1-4838-1213-7

10-217197811

Table of Contents

Name ____________________

The Alphabet

Aa 	Bb 	Cc 
Dd 	Ee 	Ff 
Gg 	Hh 	Ii 
Jj 	Kk 	Ll 
Mm 	Nn 	Oo 
Pp 	Qq 	Rr 
Ss 	Tt 	Uu 
Vv 	Ww 	Xx 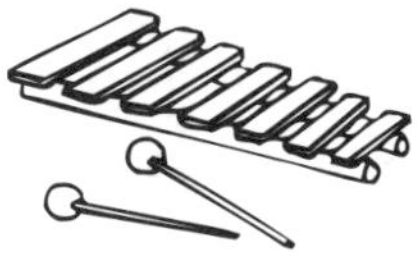
Yy 	Zz 	

Directions: Say each letter and the picture next to it aloud.

Home Practice: Review the alphabet and practice together any letter that may be especially hard for your child to say, remember, or learn.

Name ________________________________

Same and Different

Directions: In each row, put an **X** on the object that is a different color than the others.
Home Practice: Point to an object in each row. Ask your child to find or name an object in the room that is the same color.

Name________________________________

Colors

green yellow

orange red

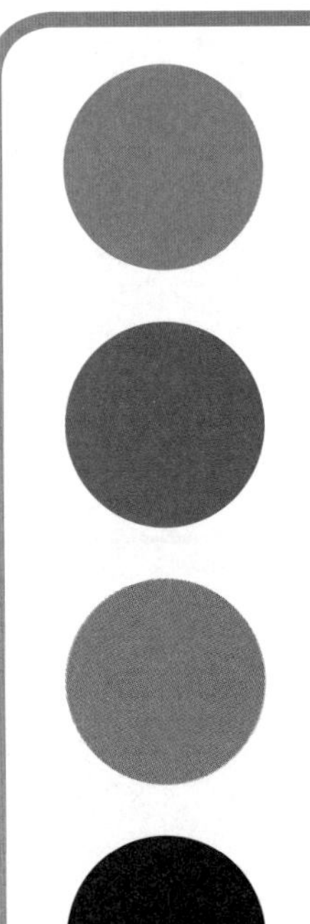

purple brown

blue black

Directions: Have students point to each color and then to each color name.
Home Practice: Ask your child to find something else in the room that matches each color.

Name ____________________

Match the Picture

Matt blows a bubble with his gum.

Tia and Erik painted a rainbow together.

Directions: Read the sentence in the box aloud. Have students circle the picture that matches the sentence.
Home Practice: Ask your child to tell a story about each series of pictures.

Name ____________________

Match the Picture

Mama Duck is mad at Baby Duck.

Mama Duck loves Baby Duck.

Mama Duck cannot find Baby Duck.

Ana takes a bath.

Ana breaks the dishes.

Ana washes the dishes.

Directions: Read the sentences in the box aloud. Have students circle the sentence that matches the picture below it.
Home Practice: Ask your child to choose one of the sentences that he or she did not circle and draw a picture to illustrate it.

Name____

Classifying

Directions: Circle the objects that go together in each box.
Home Practice: Have your child tell you how the objects that go together are related.

Name ____________________

Matching Words

 top	cap	top	top
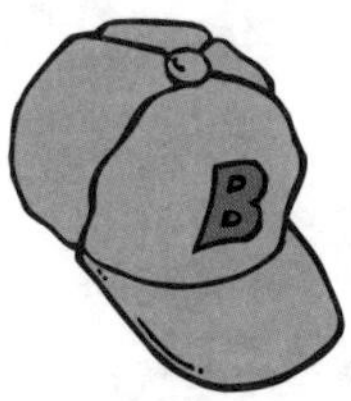 cap	cap	pig	cap
 pig	top	pig	pig
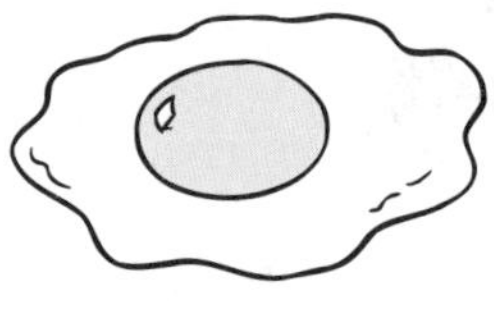 egg	egg	egg	top
 cub	cap	cub	cub

Directions: Circle the words that match the first word.
Home Practice: Have your child point to other words in the workbook that match.

Name____________________

Matching Words

do	do	you	do
you	the	you	do
smell	do	smell	smell
the	the	you	the
cake	cake	smell	cake

Directions: Circle the words that match the first word.
Home Practice: Have your child point to other words in the workbook that match.

Name____

Missing Letters

Directions: Write the missing letter in each word.
Home Practice: Have your child name the letters in each word.

Name ____________________

How Many?

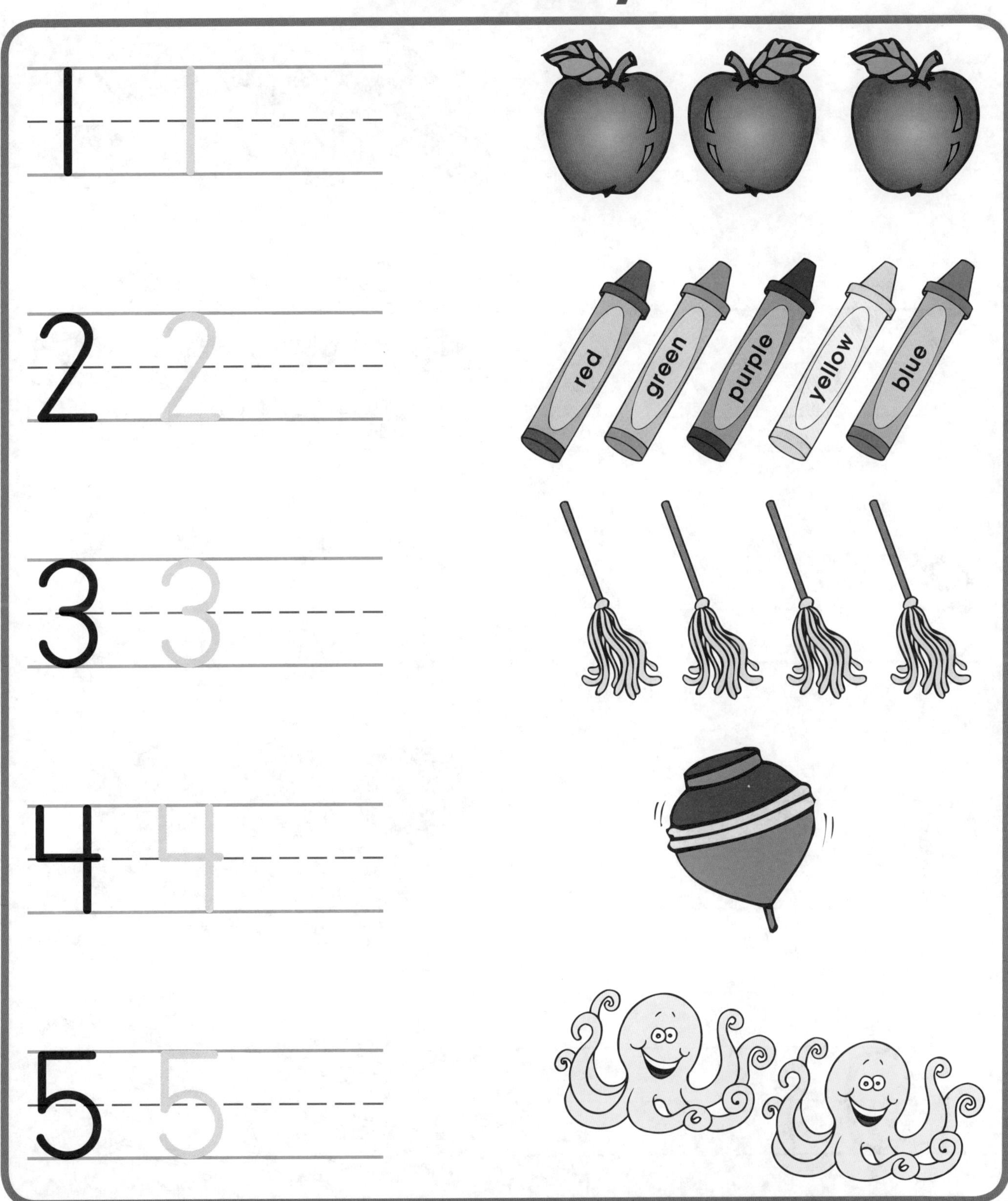

Directions: Trace each numeral and then write it. Then, draw a line from the numeral to the picture set it represents.
Home Practice: Ask your child to name the objects and count each set aloud.

Name

How Many?

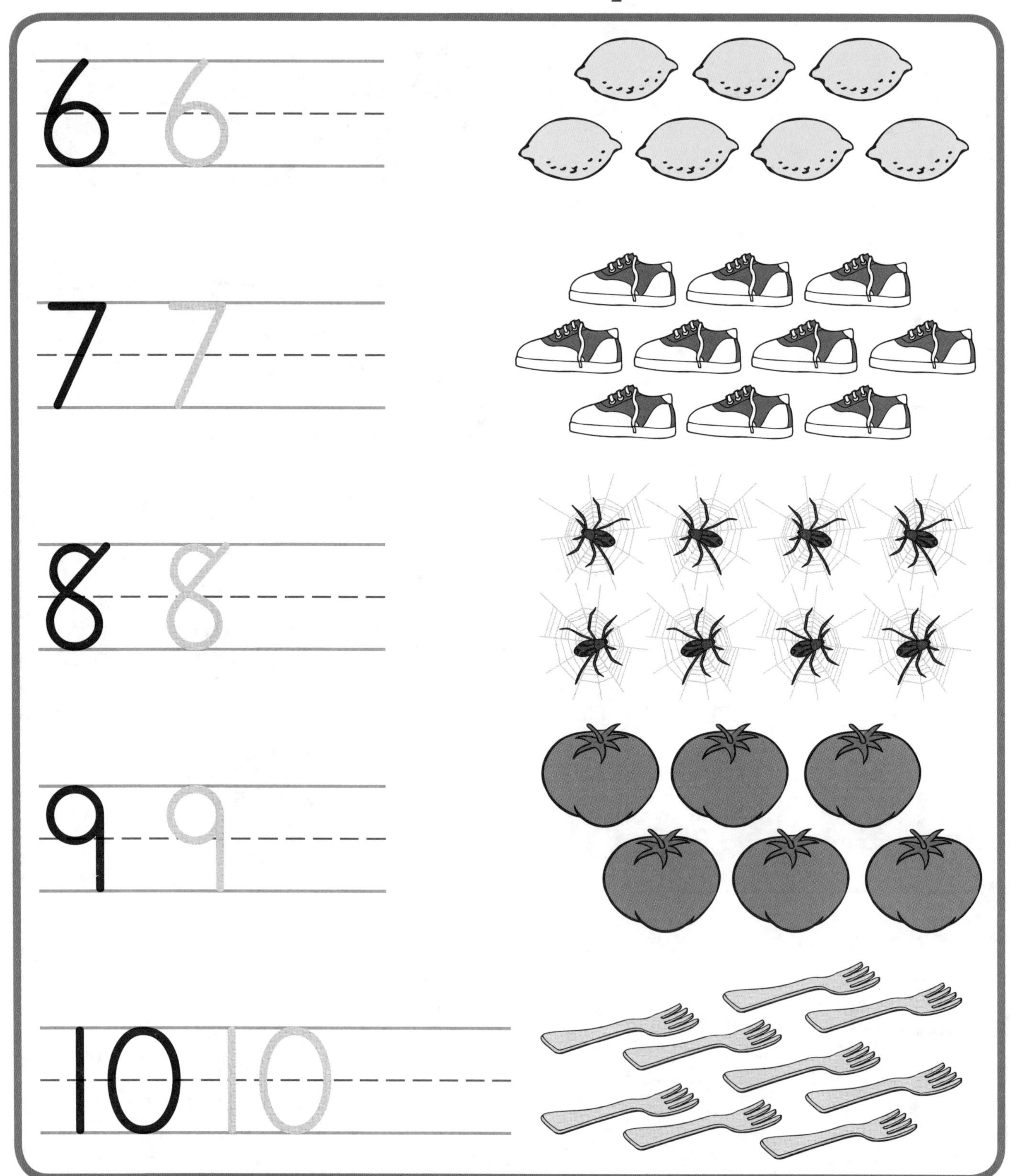

Directions: Trace each numeral and then write it. Then, draw a line from the numeral to the picture set it represents.
Home Practice: Ask your child to name the objects and count each set aloud.

Name______________________________

A Day at the Park

Directions: Discuss the picture.
Home Practice: Ask your child to look at the picture and describe what each person is doing. Ask your child what he or she would most like to do at the park.

Name

Sequencing

Directions: Write **1** below the picture that happened first, **2** below the picture that happened next, and **3** below the picture that happened last.

Home Practice: Have your child tell each story in the correct sequence.

Name ______________________

Letters

Aa				Bb
A	A	N	C	A
a	e	a	o	a
B	P	B	C	B
b	g	d	b	b

Directions: In each row, circle the matching letters.
Home Practice: Point to a circled letter in each row. Have your child find each letter somewhere else in the workbook.

Name

Sounds

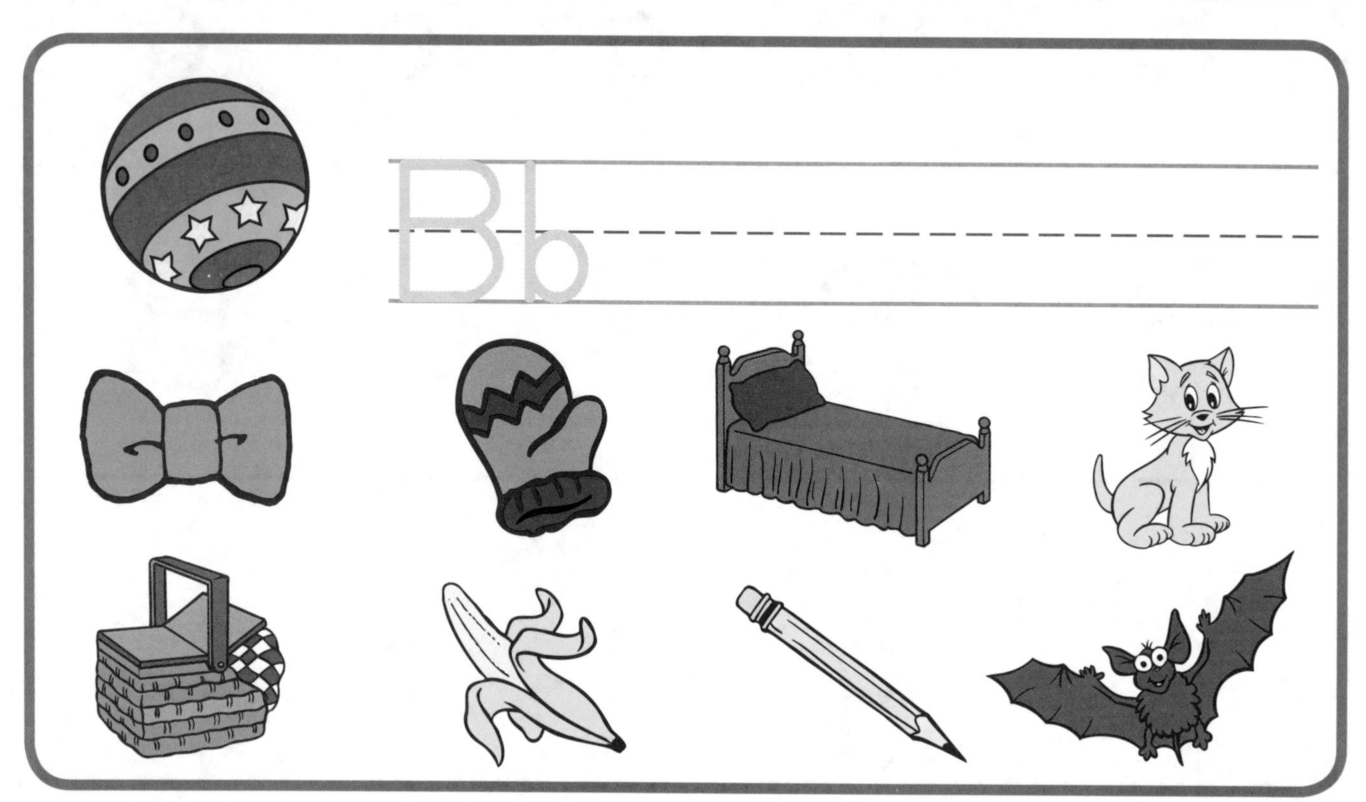

Directions: Trace the letters and write them. Name each picture. Circle each picture whose name begins with the same sound as the first picture.

Home Practice: Ask your child to name other words that begin with the same sound.

Name

The Sounds of A and B

Directions: Trace the letters and write them. Write the letter **A** below the pictures that begin with that sound. Then, do the same thing for **B**.

Home Practice: Have your child find pictures that begin with **A** and **B**.

Name

Sounds: A

Directions: Trace the letters and write them. Circle each picture whose name has the sound you hear in the middle of *hat*.
Home Practice: Ask your child to point to and name three pictures. Then, say each of these words, and have your child tell you whether it has the same middle sound as *hat*.

Name ___________________________________

Apple Picking

Directions: Discuss the picture.
Home Practice: Ask your child to look at the picture and describe what each person is doing.

Name

Letters

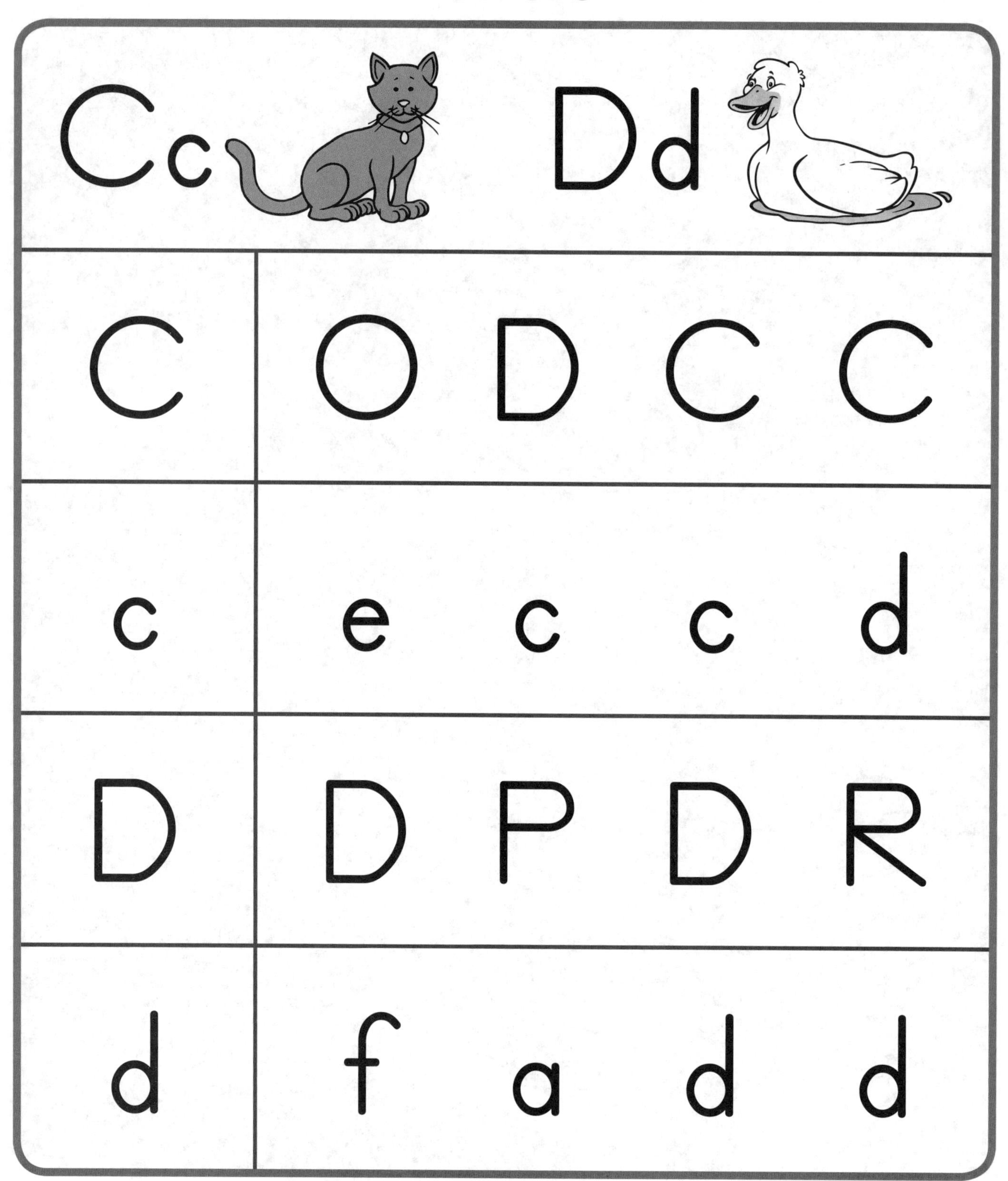

Directions: In each row, circle the matching letters.
Home Practice: Point to a circled letter in each row. Have your child find each letter somewhere else in the workbook.

Name

Sounds

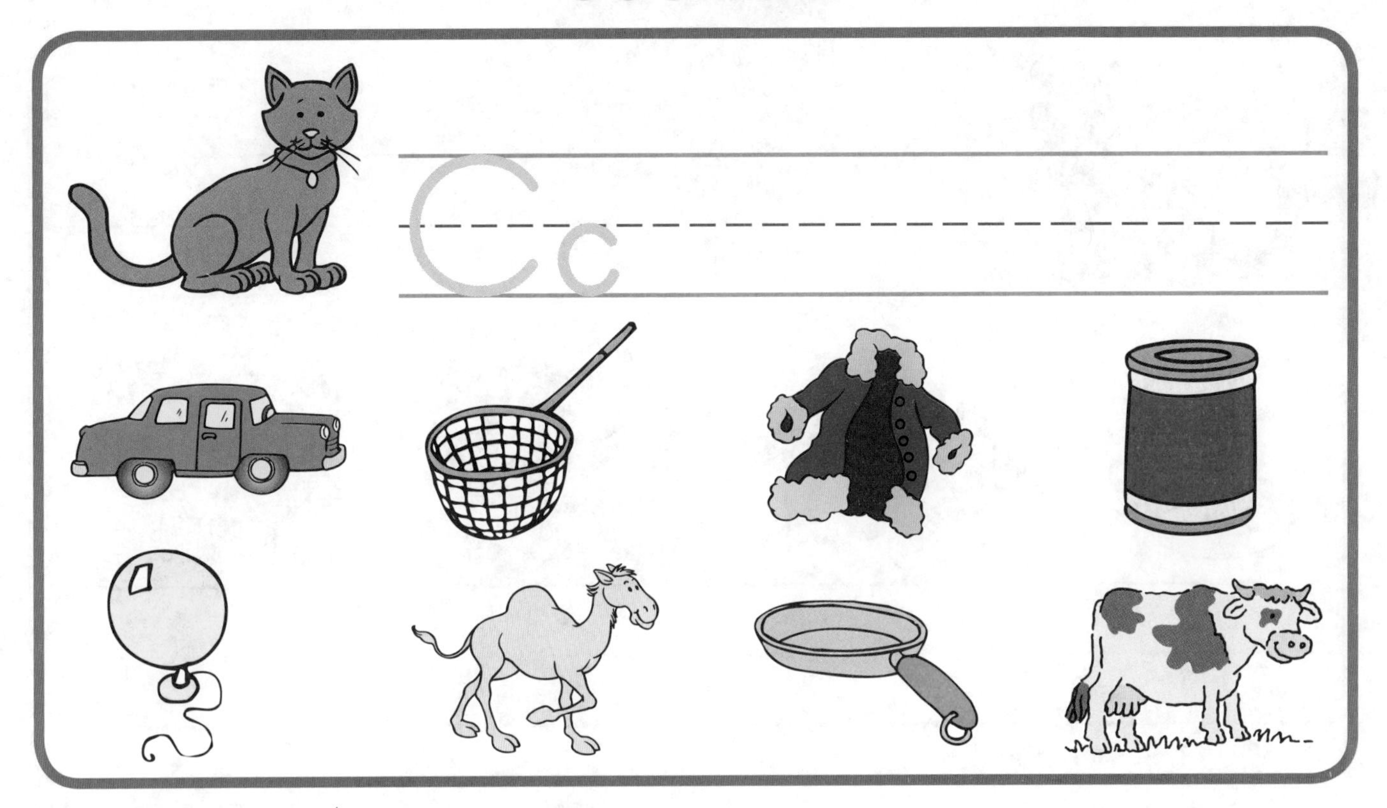

Directions: Trace the letters and write them. Name each picture. Circle each picture whose name begins with the same sound as the first picture.
Home Practice: Ask your child to name other words that begin with the same sound.

Name

Sounds: C and D

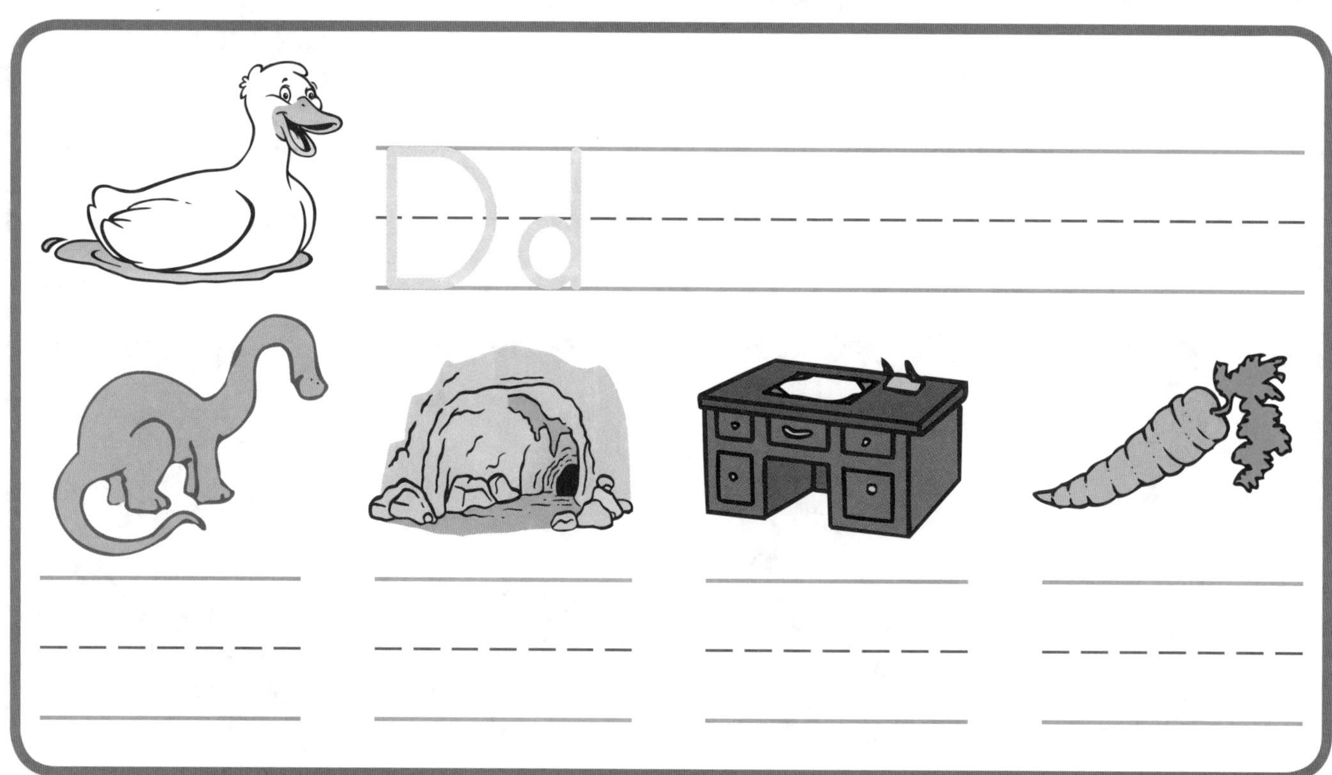

Directions: Trace the letters and write them. Write the letter **C** below the pictures that begin with that sound. Then, do the same thing for **D**.

Home Practice: Have your child find pictures that begin with **C** and **D**.

Name

Sounds: A, B, C, and D

Directions: Look at the first letter in each row. Circle each picture whose name begins with the same sound.
Home Practice: Have your child point to each letter and name another object whose name begins with the same sound.

Name____

Bedtime

Directions: Discuss the pictures.
Home Practice: Ask your child to tell a story about what is happening in the pictures shown.

Name

Letters

Ee

Ff

E	E	F	E	T
e	g	c	e	e
F	T	F	H	N
f	f	t	l	f

Directions: In each row, circle the matching letters.

Home Practice: Point to a circled letter in each row. Have your child find each letter somewhere else in the workbook.

Name

Sounds

Directions: Trace the letters and write them. Name each picture. Circle each picture whose name begins with the same sound as the first picture.

Home Practice: Ask your child to name other words that begin with the same sound.

Name

The Sounds of E and F

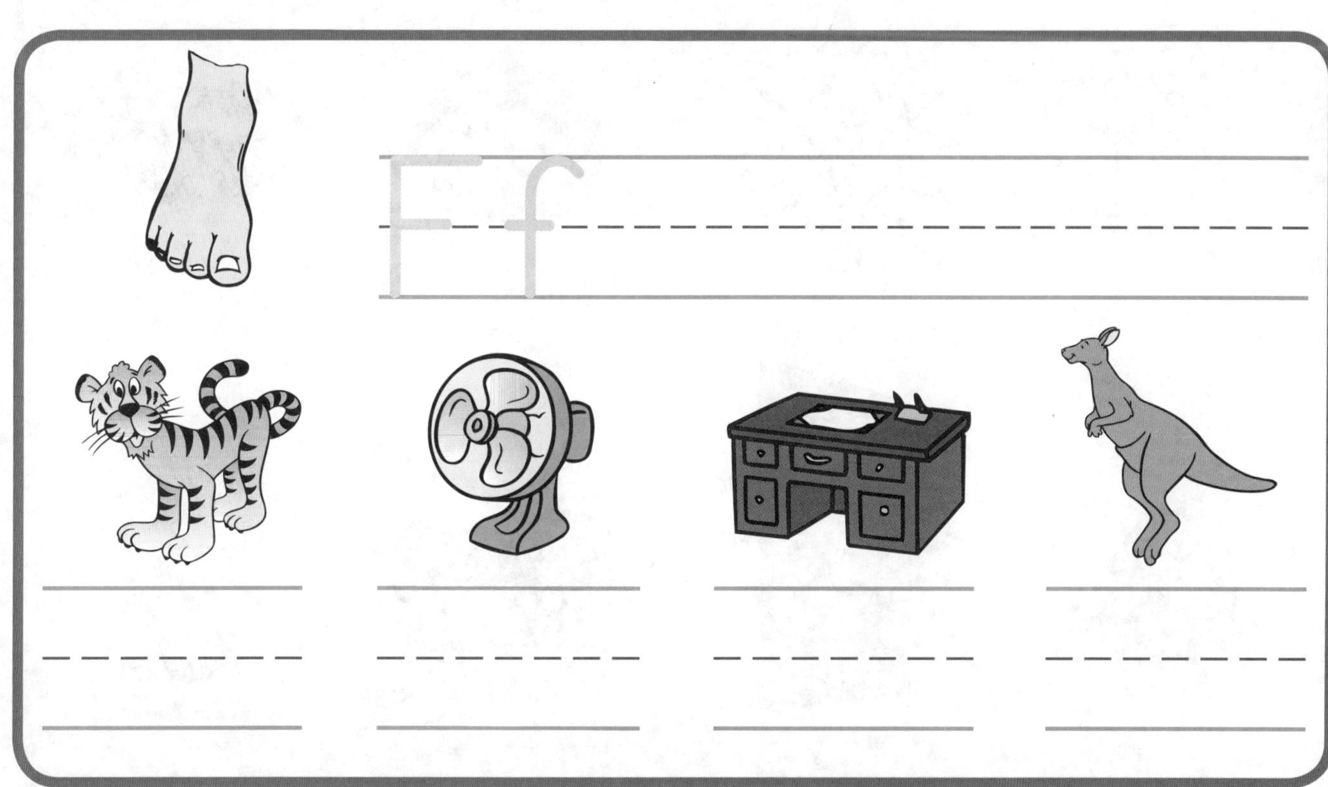

Directions: Trace the letters and write them. Write the letter **E** below the pictures that begin with that sound. Then, do the same thing for **F**.

Home Practice: Have your child find pictures that begin with **E** and **F**.

Name ____________________

Sounds: E

Directions: Trace the letters and write them. Circle each picture whose name has the sound you hear in the middle of *bed*.
Home Practice: Ask your child to point to and name three pictures. Then, say each of these words, and have your child tell you whether it has the same middle sound as *bed*.

Name___________________________________

Classifying

Directions: In each row, circle the three objects that belong together.

Home Practice: Have your child name the pictures in each row that are circled. Then, have your child tell how the objects are alike and why they go together.

Name ____________________

Practice Fire Drill

Directions: Discuss the pictures.

Home Practice: Have your child tell what is happening in the pictures shown. Discuss a fire drill at home.

Name

Classifying

Directions: Draw a line connecting the objects that go together in each box.
Home Practice: Have your child tell you how the objects that go together are related.

Name

Letters

Gg Hh

G	C G O G
g	t j g g
H	H F H K
h	k t h h

Directions: In each row, circle the matching letters.
Home Practice: Point to a circled letter in each row. Have your child find each letter somewhere else in the workbook.

Name________________________________

Sounds

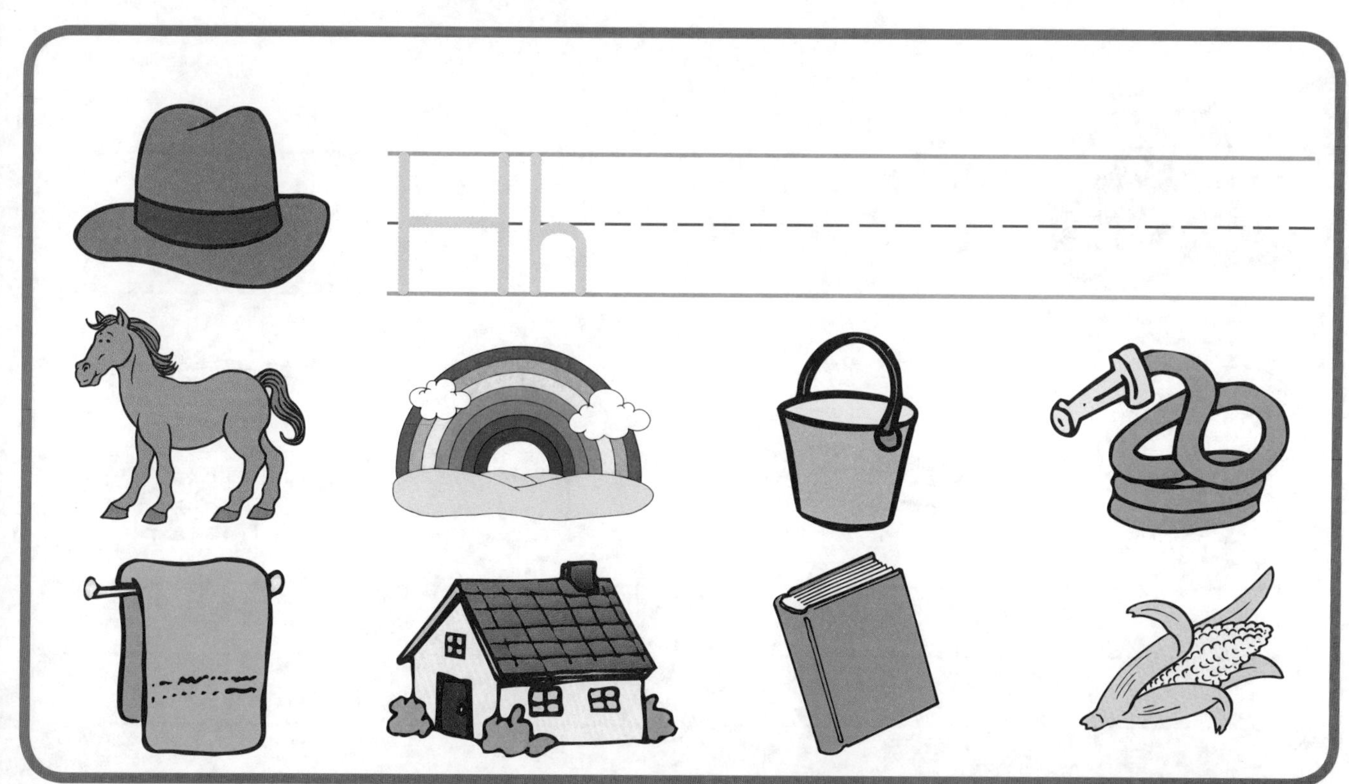

Directions: Trace the letters and write them. Name each picture. Circle each picture whose name begins with the same sound as the first picture.

Home Practice: Ask your child to name other words that begin with the same sound.

Name

The Sounds of G and H

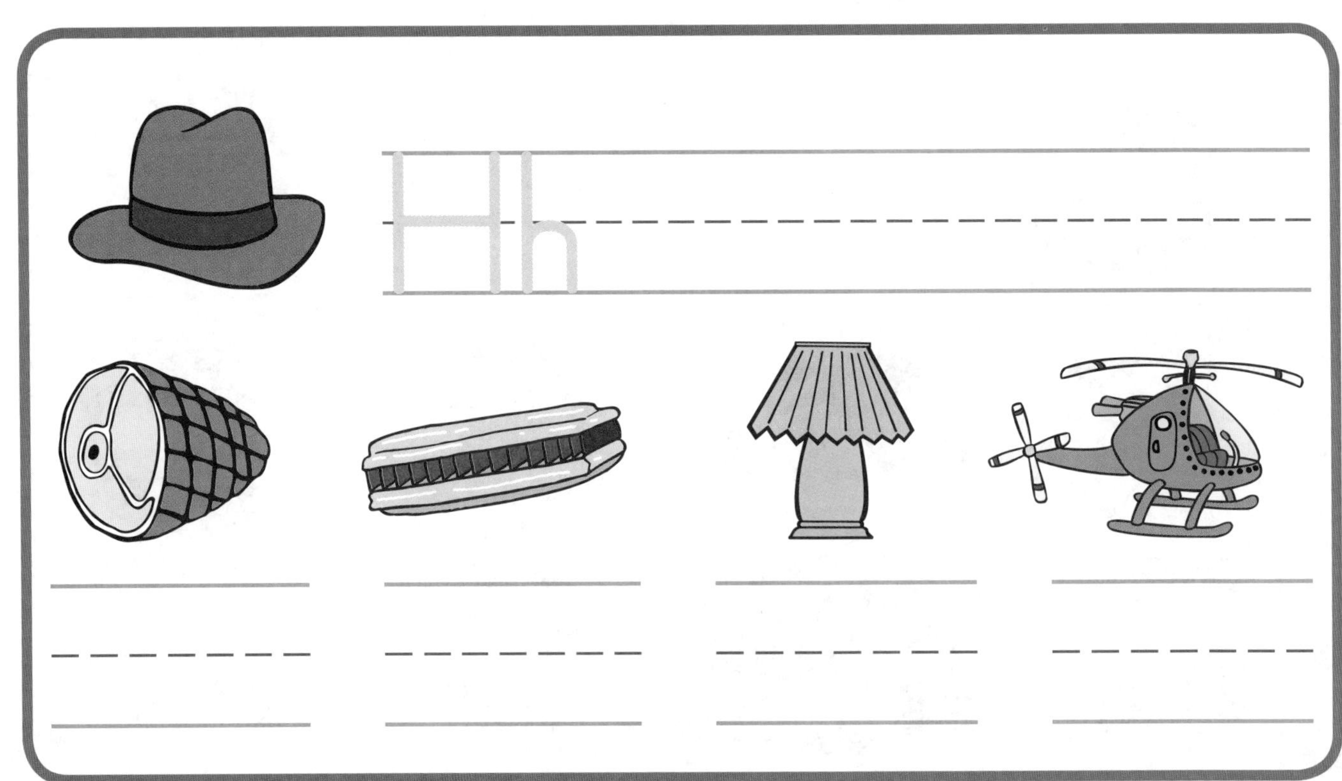

Directions: Trace the letters and write them. Write the letter **G** below the pictures that begin with that sound. Then, do the same thing for **H**.

Home Practice: Have your child find pictures that begin with **G** and **H**.

Name

Sounds: E, F, G, and H

Directions: Look at the first letter in each row. Circle each picture whose name begins with the same sound.
Home Practice: Have your child point to each letter and name another object whose name begins with the same sound.

Name ______________________________

Happy Birthday to You

Directions: Discuss the picture.
Home Practice: Have your child look at the picture and describe what each person is doing.

Name ____________________

Sequencing

Directions: Write **1** below the picture that happened first, **2** below the picture that happened next, and **3** below the picture that happened last.

Home Practice: Have your child tell each story in the correct sequence.

Name ____________________

Letters

Ii	ink	Jj	
I	L N I I		
i	i j l i		
J	D J G J		
j	j y v j		

Directions: In each row, circle the matching letters.
Home Practice: Point to a circled letter in each row. Have your child find each letter somewhere else in the workbook.

Name________________________________

Sounds

Directions: Trace the letters and write them. Name each picture. Circle each picture whose name begins with the same sound as the first picture.

Home Practice: Ask your child to name other words that begin with the same sound.

Name

Sounds: I and J

Directions: Trace the letters and write them. Write the letter **I** below the pictures that begin with that sound. Then, do the same thing for **J**.

Home Practice: Have your child find pictures that begin with **I** and **J**.

Name

Sounds: I

Directions: Trace the letters and write them. Name the pictures. Circle each picture whose name has the sound you hear in the middle of *pig*.

Home Practice: Ask your child to point to and name three pictures. Then, say each of these words, and have your child tell you whether it has the same middle sound as *pig*.

Name

Classifying

Directions: Circle the three objects that belong together in each row.
Home Practice: Have your child tell how the circled objects are related to each other.

Name ______________________________

Wintertime

Directions: Discuss the picture.
Home Practice: Ask your child to look at the picture and describe what each person is doing. Ask your child what he or she would most like to be doing if part of this scene.

Name ________________________________

Big and Small

Directions: In each row, circle the object that is big. Make a line under the object that is small.
Home Practice: Discuss the differences in size with your child.

Name ____________________

Letters

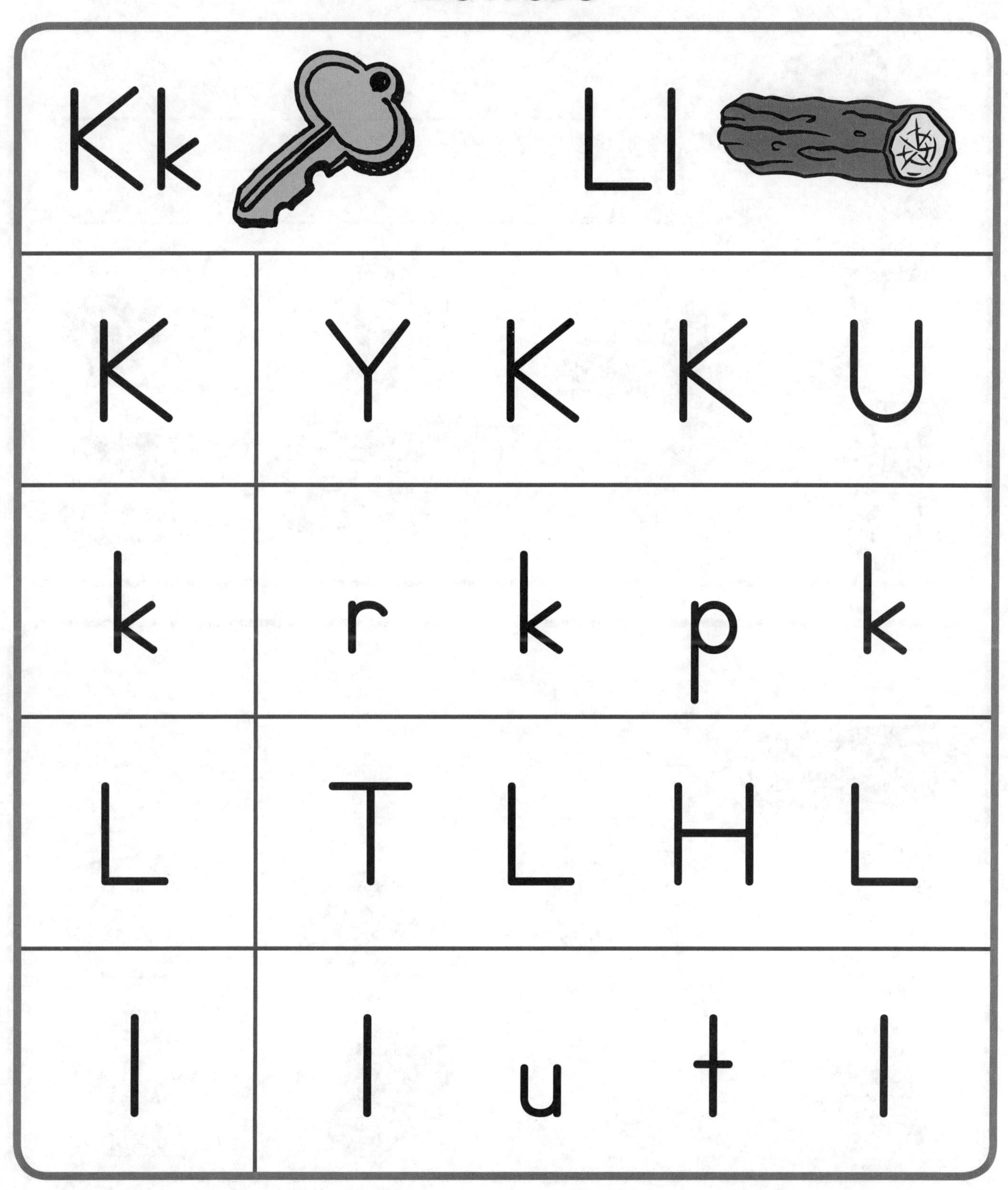

Directions: In each row, circle the matching letters.
Home Practice: Point to a circled letter in each row. Have your child find each letter somewhere else in the workbook.

Name ______________________________

Sounds

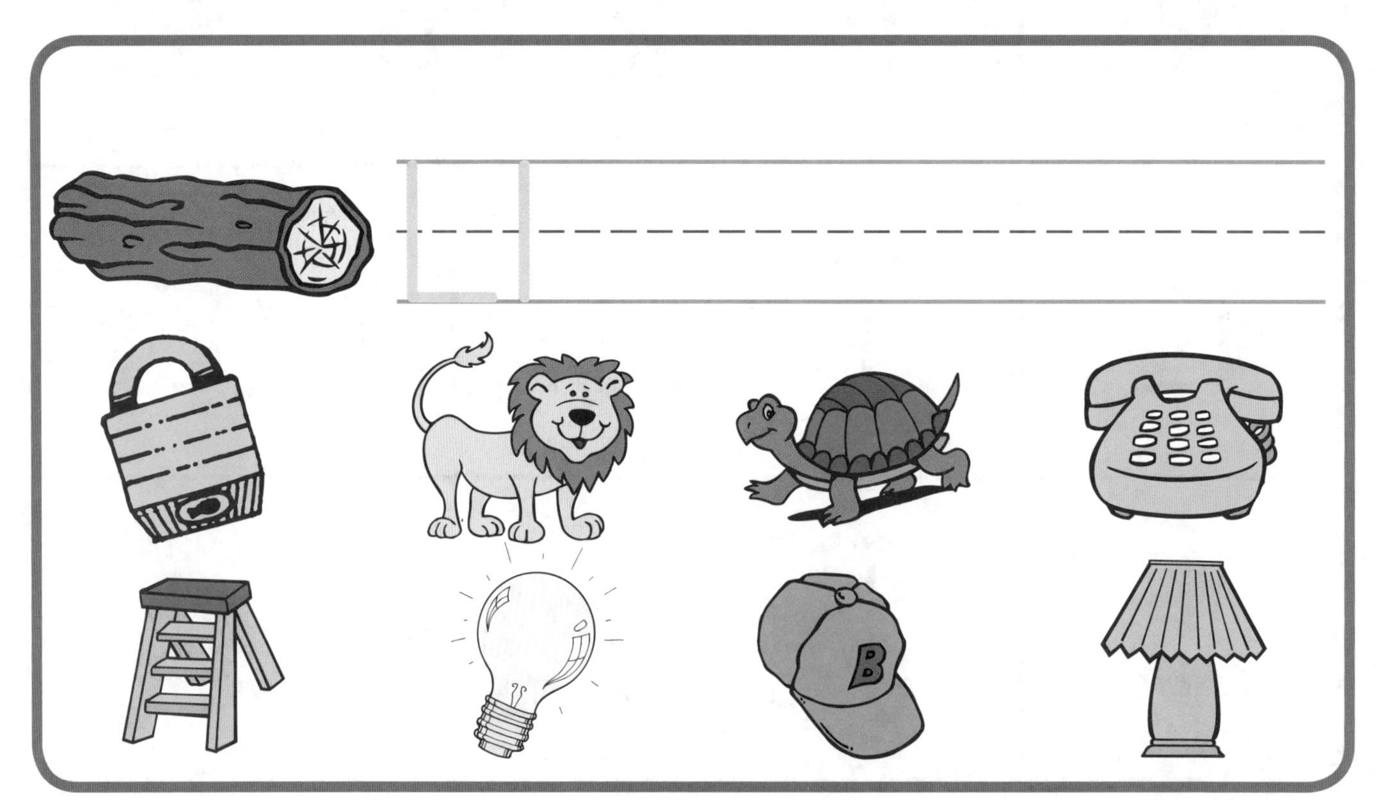

Directions: Trace the letters and write them. Name each picture. Circle each picture whose name begins with the same sound as the first picture.

Home Practice: Ask your child to name other words that begin with the same sound.

Name______________________________

Sounds: K and L

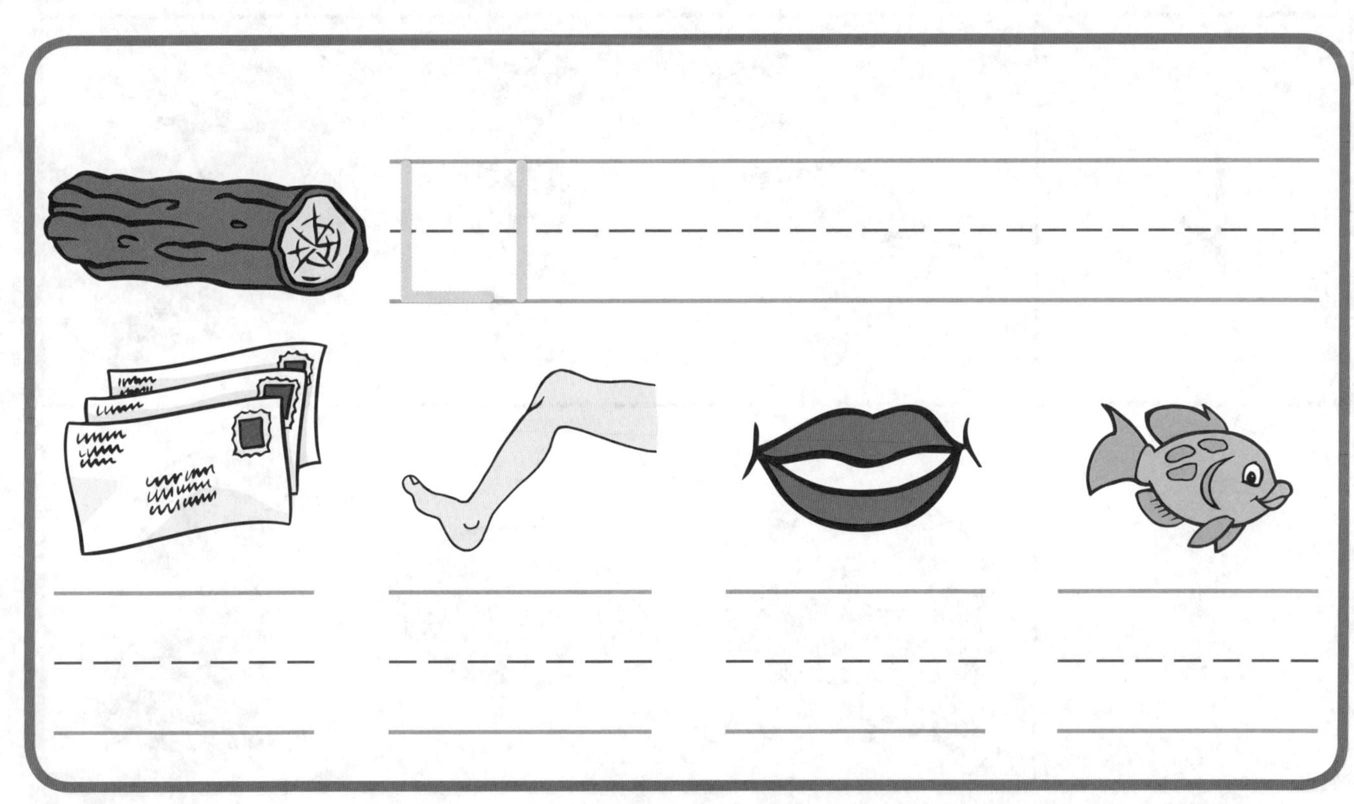

Directions: Trace the letters and write them. Write the letter **K** below the pictures that begin with that sound. Then, do the same thing for **L**.
Home Practice: Have your child find pictures that begin with **K** and **L**.

Name ______________________________

Sounds: I, J, K, and L

Directions: Look at the first letter in each row. Circle each picture whose name begins with the same sound.
Home Practice: Have your child point to each letter and name another object whose name begins with the same sound.

Name ______________________________

Let's Go Fly a Kite!

Directions: Discuss the pictures.
Home Practice: Have your child tell what is happening in the pictures shown.

Name______________________________________

Classifying

Directions: Circle one picture that belongs with the first picture in each row.
Home Practice: Have your child tell you how the objects he or she chose belong together.

Name

Letters

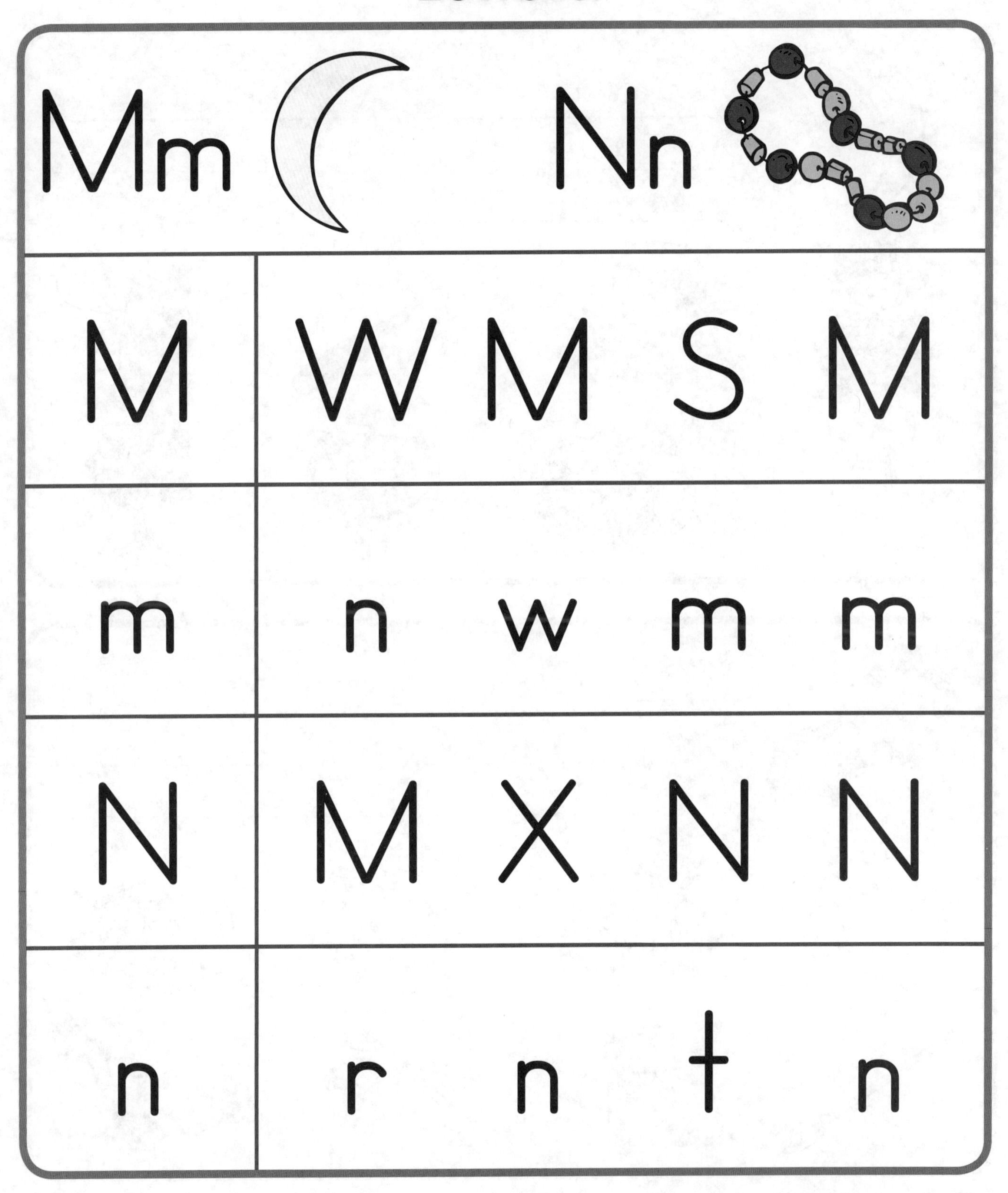

Directions: In each row, circle the matching letters.
Home Practice: Point to a circled letter in each row. Have your child find each letter somewhere else in the workbook.

Name

Sounds

Directions: Trace the letters and write them. Name each picture. Circle each picture whose name begins with the same sound as the first picture.

Home Practice: Ask your child to name other words that begin with the same sound.

Name

Sounds: M and N

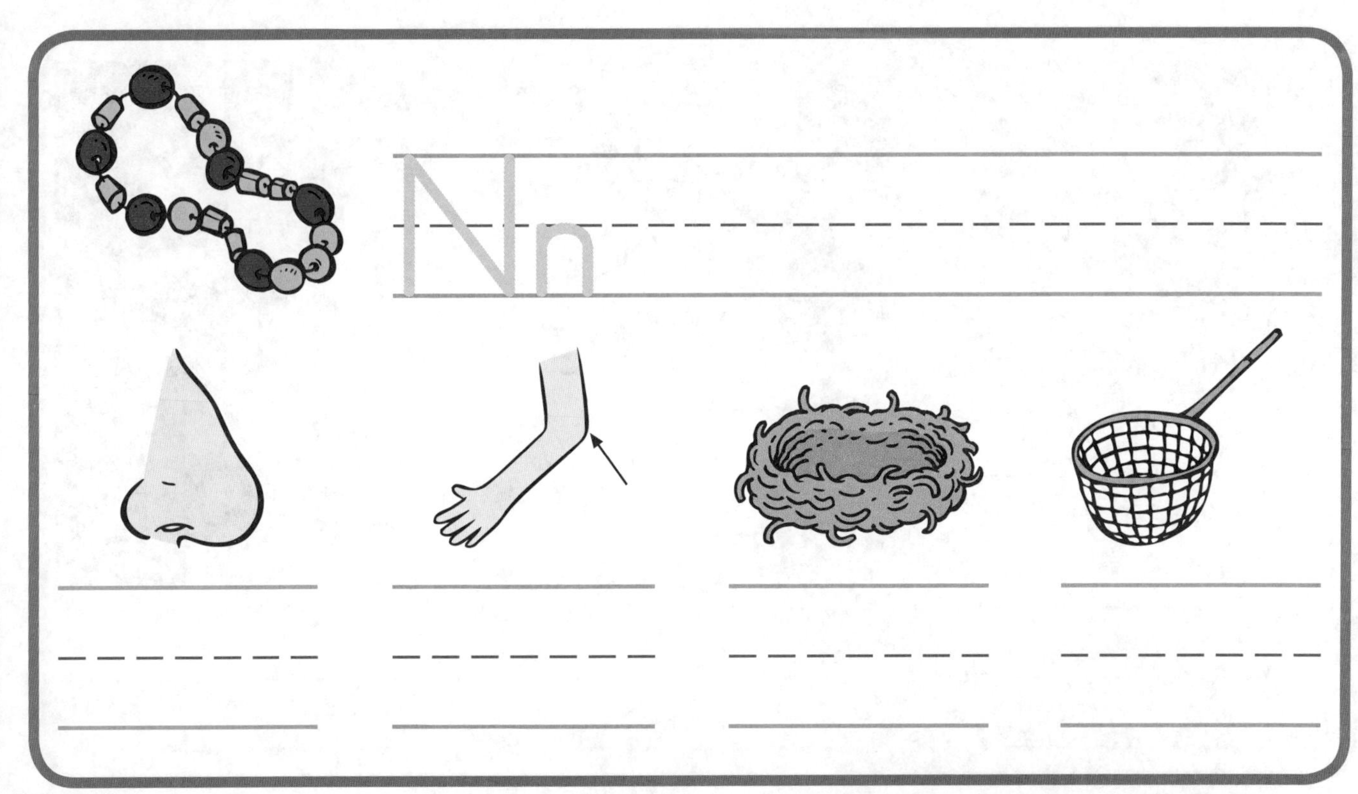

Directions: Trace the letters and write them. Write the letter **M** below the pictures that begin with that sound. Then, do the same thing for **N**.
Home Practice: Have your child find pictures that begin with **M** and **N**.

Name

Sequencing

Directions: Write **1** below the picture that happened first, **2** below the picture that happened next, and **3** below the picture that happened last.
Home Practice: Have your child tell each story in the correct sequence.

Name ____________________

A Day at the Beach

Directions: Discuss the picture.

Home Practice: Ask your child to look at the picture and explain what the children are doing. Have your child tell what the children in the picture might be thinking or feeling.

Name ____________________

Rhyming Words

Directions: Draw lines between pictures that rhyme.
Home Practice: Have your child name other objects that rhyme.

Name________________________________

Classifying

Directions: In each row, circle the three objects that belong together.
Home Practice: Have your child tell how the circled objects are related to one another.

Name ______________________

Letters

Oo	Pp

O	Q	O	U	O
o	c	g	o	o
P	R	P	F	B
p	q	p	r	p

Directions: In each row, circle the matching letters.
Home Practice: Point to a circled letter in each row. Have your child find each letter somewhere else in the workbook.

Name

Sounds

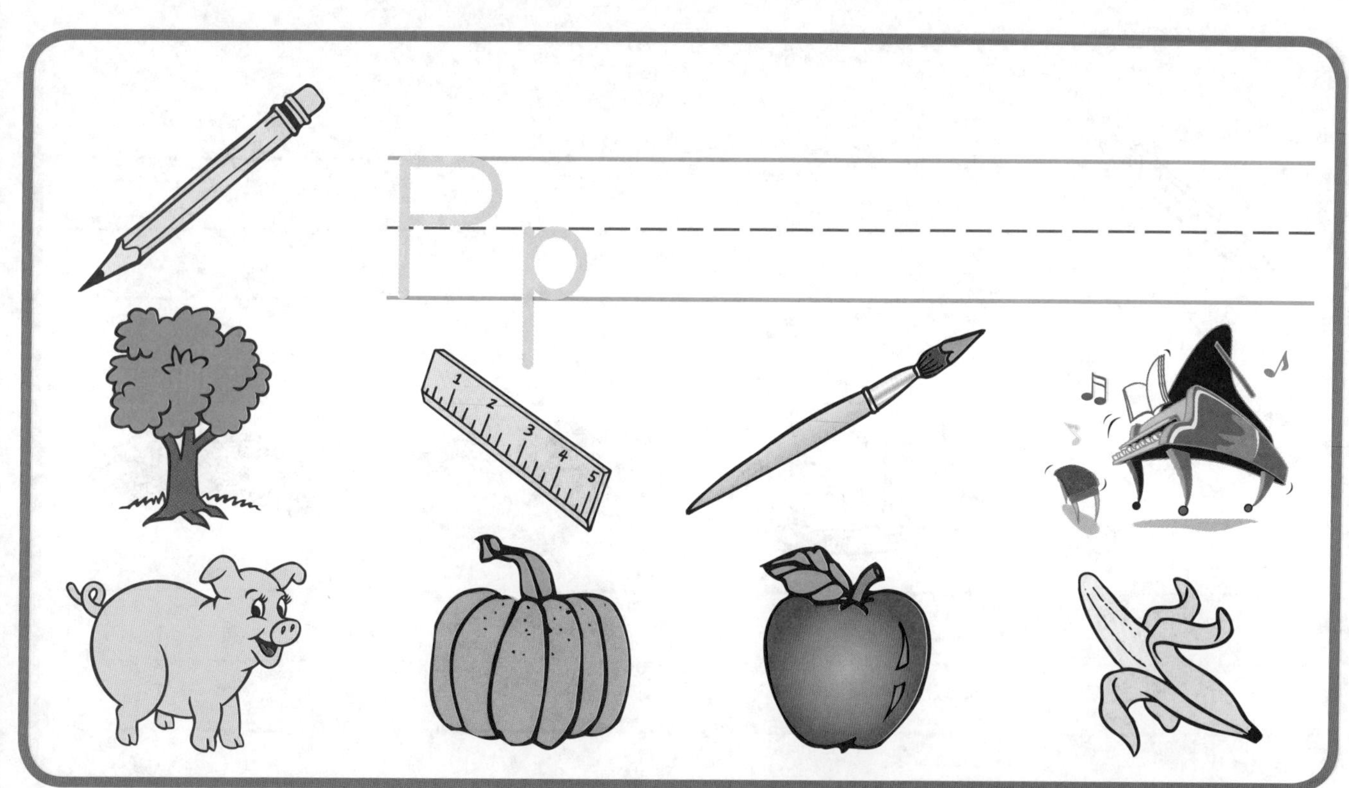

Directions: Trace the letters and write them. Name each picture. Circle each picture whose name begins with the same sound as the first picture.
Home Practice: Ask your child to name other words that begin with the same sound.

Name ______________________________

Sounds: O and P

Directions: Trace the letters and write them. Write the letter **O** below the pictures that begin with that sound. Then, do the same thing for **P**.
Home Practice: Have your child find pictures that begin with **O** and **P**.

Name ______________________________

Sounds: O

Directions: Trace the letters and write them. Name the pictures. Circle each picture whose name has the sound you hear in the middle of *top*.

Home Practice: Ask your child to point to and name three pictures. Then, say each of these words, and have your child tell you whether it has the same middle sound as *top*.

Name____________________

Sounds: M, N, O, and P

Directions: Look at the first letter in each row. Circle each picture whose name begins with the same sound.
Home Practice: Have your child point to each letter and name another object whose name begins with the same sound.

Name

The First Day of School

Directions: Discuss the picture.
Home Practice: Ask your child to look at the picture and name some of the objects in the picture. Have your child tell what the people in the picture might be thinking or feeling.

Name

Letters

Qq Rr

Q	Q	O	C	Q
q	g	q	p	q
R	R	P	R	F
r	y	r	r	w

Directions: In each row, circle the matching letters.
Home Practice: Point to a circled letter in each row. Have your child find each letter somewhere else in the workbook.

Name ______________________________

Sounds

Directions: Trace the letters and write them. Name each picture. Circle each picture whose name begins with the same sound as the first picture.

Home Practice: Ask your child to name other words that begin with the same sound.

Name ______________________________

Sounds: Q and R

Directions: Trace the letters and write them. Write the letter **Q** below the pictures that begin with that sound. Then, do the same thing for **R**.

Home Practice: Have your child find pictures that begin with **Q** and **R**.

Name____

Position Words

Directions: Circle the picture that shows the cat above. Circle the picture that shows the truck next to. Circle the picture that shows the book on the bottom.

Home Practice: Point to pictures at random, and have your child describe them.

Name ________________________________

A Day on the Farm

Directions: Talk about the picture.
Home Practice: Ask your child to look at the picture and tell about what is happening.

Name ______________________________

Rhyming Words

Directions: Circle each picture that rhymes with the first picture.
Home Practice: Have your child name other objects that rhyme.

Name________________________________

Letters

Ss	Tt

S	G	S	Y	S
s	t	q	s	s
T	L	T	Y	T
t	l	t	y	t

Directions: In each row, circle the matching letters.
Home Practice: Point to a circled letter in each row. Have your child find each letter somewhere else in the workbook.

Name

Sounds

Directions: Trace the letters and write them. Circle each picture whose name begins with the same sound as the first picture.
Home Practice: Ask your child to name other words that begin with the same sound.

Name____

Sounds: S and T

Directions: Trace the letters and write them. Write the letter **S** below the pictures that begin with that sound. Then, do the same thing for **T**.

Home Practice: Have your child find pictures that begin with **S** and **T**.

Name

Sounds: Q, R, S, and T

Directions: Look at the first letter in each row. Circle each picture whose name begins with the same sound.

Home Practice: Have your child point to each letter and name another item found at school whose name begins with the same sound.

Name____

Watch It Grow!

Directions: Talk about the pictures.

Home Practice: Ask your child to look at the pictures and tell about what is happening. Ask your child if he or she has ever planted anything.

Name______________________________________

Same and Different

Directions: Circle the picture that is the most different in each row.
Home Practice: Point to different pictures in the same row. Ask your child to tell how they are alike and different.

Name ____________________

Letters

Uu Vv

U	V	U	W	U
u	u	n	u	v
V	Y	W	V	V
v	a	v	u	w

Directions: In each row, circle the matching letters.
Home Practice: Point to a circled letter in each row. Have your child find each letter somewhere else in the workbook.

Name ____________________

Sounds

Directions: Trace the letters and write them. Name each picture. Circle each picture whose name begins with the same sound as the first picture.
Home Practice: Ask your child to name other words that begin with the same sound.

Name

Sounds: U and V

Directions: Trace the letters and write them. Write the letter **U** below the pictures that begin with that sound. Then, do the same thing for **V**.

Home Practice: Have your child find pictures that begin with **U** and **V**.

Name ____________________

Sounds: U

Directions: Name the pictures. Circle each picture whose name has the sound you hear in the middle of *sun*.
Home Practice: Have your child name other words that have the same middle sound as *sun*.

Name________________________________

Start and Finish

Directions: Circle the picture in each row that would be the result of the first picture.
Home Practice: Point to a different picture on the page and ask your child to describe it.

Name ______________________________

Rainy Days

Directions: Talk about the picture.
Home Practice: Ask your child to look at the picture and tell about what each person is doing.

Name ________________________________

Position Words

Directions: Circle each picture that your teacher identifies (left, right, up, down, in, out).
Home Practice: Point to pictures at random, and have your child describe them.

Name

Letters

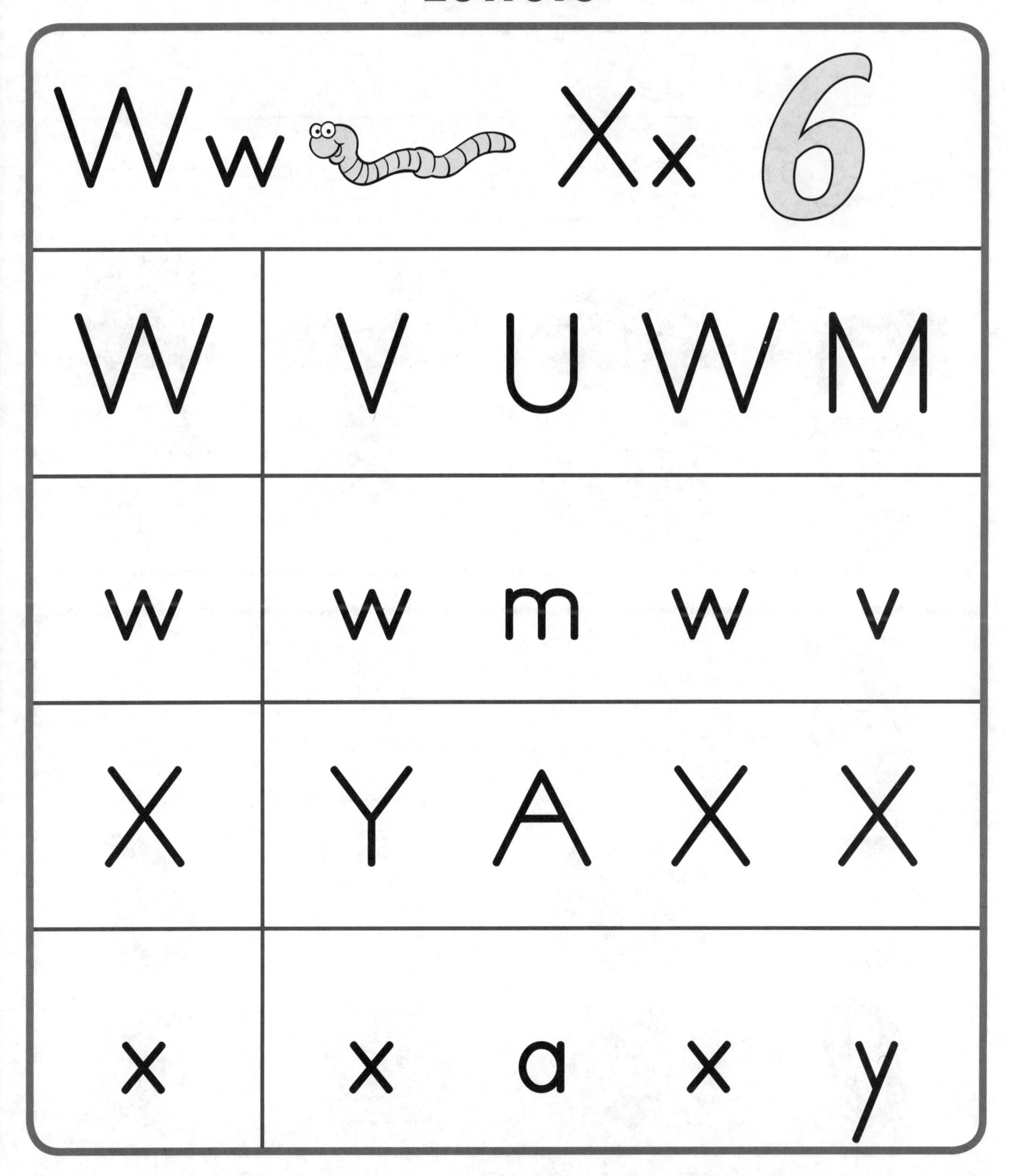

Directions: In each row, circle the matching letters.
Home Practice: Point to a circled letter in each row. Have your child find each letter somewhere else in the workbook.

Name ___________________________

Sounds

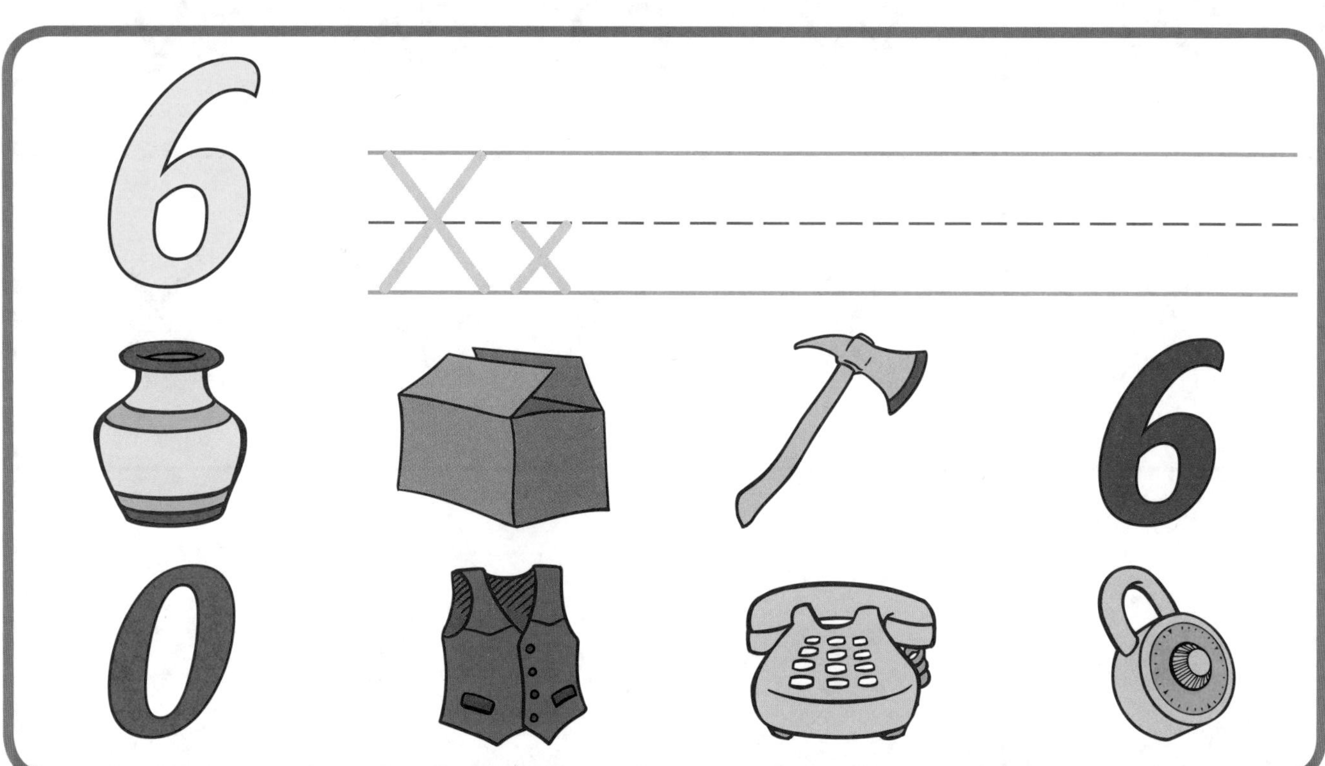

Directions: Trace the letters and write them. Name each picture. Circle each picture whose name begins with the same sound as the first picture in the top box. Then, circle each picture whose name ends with the same sound as the first picture in the bottom box.
Home Practice: Ask your child to name other words that begin with the same sound.

Name

Sounds: W and X

Directions: Trace the letters and write them. Write the letter **W** below the pictures that begin with that sound. Then, write the letter **X** below the pictures that end with that sound.

Home Practice: Have your child find pictures that begin with **W** and end with **X**.

Name ______________________________

Waterslide!

Directions: Talk about the picture.
Home Practice: Ask your child to look at the picture and tell what the different children are doing and may be feeling. Which child would they most like to be in the picture? Why?

Name

Letters

Yy Zz

Y	V N Y Y
y	y f y v
Z	A Z E Z
z	s z z n

Directions: In each row, circle the matching letters.
Home Practice: Point to a circled letter in each row. Have your child find each letter somewhere else in the workbook.

Name

Sounds

Directions: Trace the letters and write them. Name each picture. Circle each picture whose name begins with the same sound as the first picture.

Home Practice: Ask your child to name other words that begin with the same sound.

Name

Sounds: Y and Z

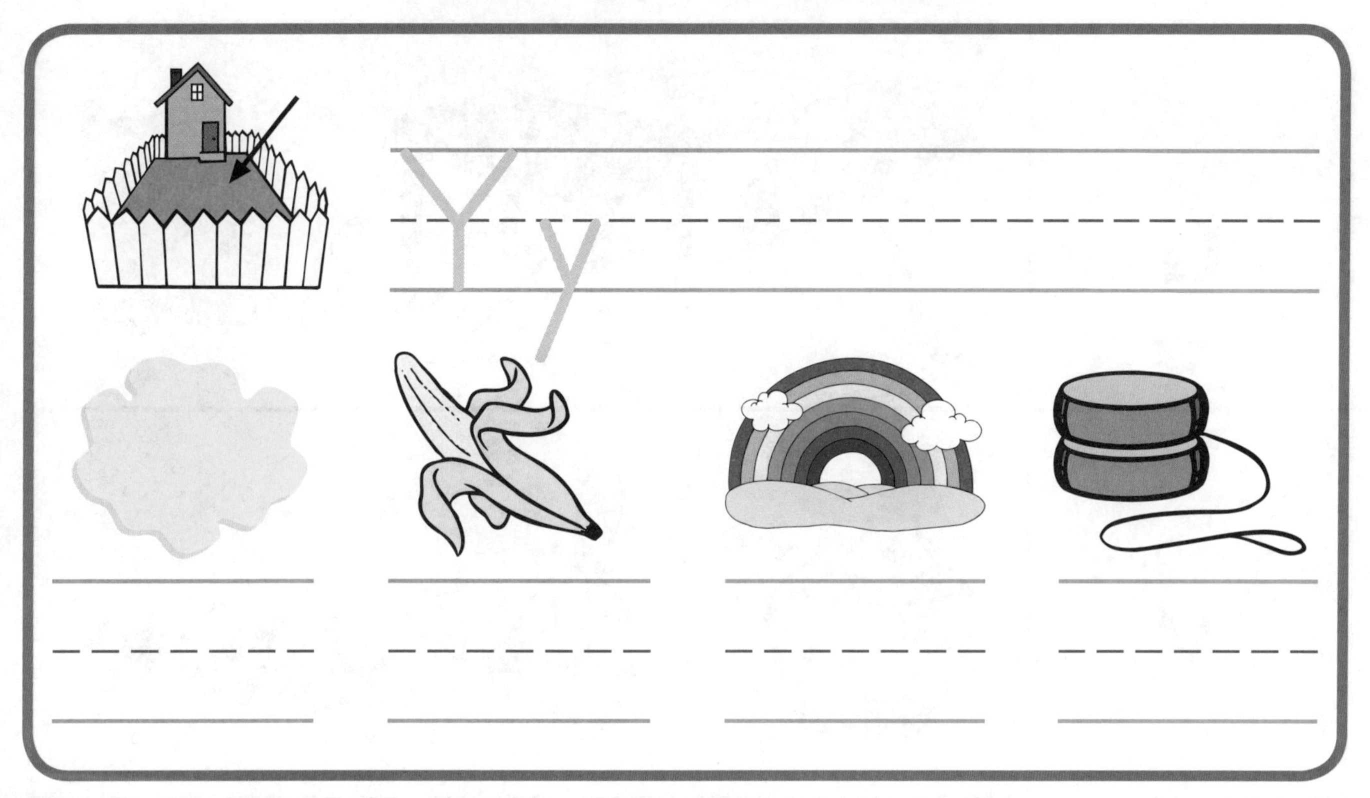

Directions: Trace the letters and write them. Write the letter **Y** below the pictures that begin with that sound. Then, do the same thing for **Z**.

Home Practice: Have your child find pictures that begin with **Y** and **Z**.

Name ____________________

Sounds: U, V, W, and Y

Directions: Look at the first letter in each row. Circle each picture whose name begins with the same sound.
Home Practice: Have your child point to each letter and name another object whose name begins with the same sound.

Name

Match It Up

	bog	dog	hog
	star	far	car
	bat	bit	bet
	peg	pug	pig

Directions: Circle the word that matches each picture. Then, write the word on the line.
Home Practice: Have your child tell you a rhyming word for each word he or she circled.

Name ____________________

Letter Sounds

b

p

r

m

f

w

s

h

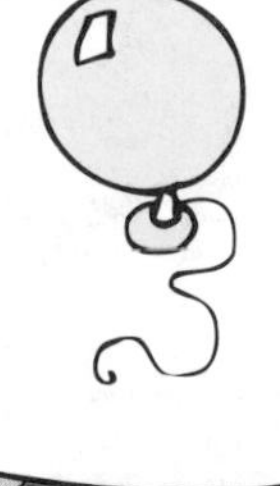

Directions: Draw a line from the letter to the picture whose name starts with that sound.
Home Practice: Have your child tell you a rhyming word for each word he or she circled.

Name

Rhyme Time

box

hook

car

wig

hat

man

toy

Directions: Draw a line from each picture to the word it rhymes with.
Home Practice: Ask your child to name other words that rhyme with each picture.

Meet Max

Meet Max.

Who is Max? What do you think he is like?

Max is big.

How do you think the other animal feels sitting next to Max?

Max is tall.

Meet Max.

How do you think Max and the other animals feel?

Picture Interpretation and Guided Reading (for all stories): Introduce students to Max, a playful puppy who is the main character of the following stories. Encourage students to look at the pictures and tell what is happening. Have them relate the events to their own experiences. Ask them to read the story silently. Help them with new words. Then, have students read the story aloud.

Name ____________________

I. B

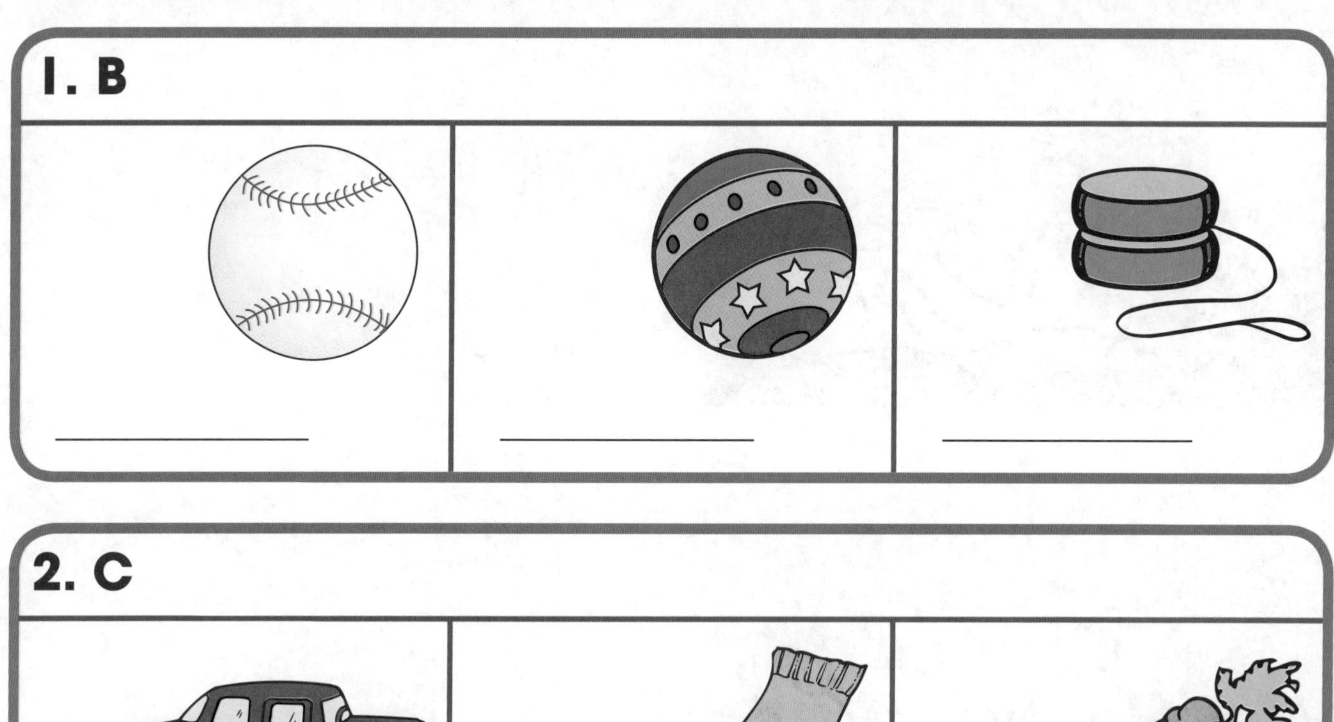

2. C

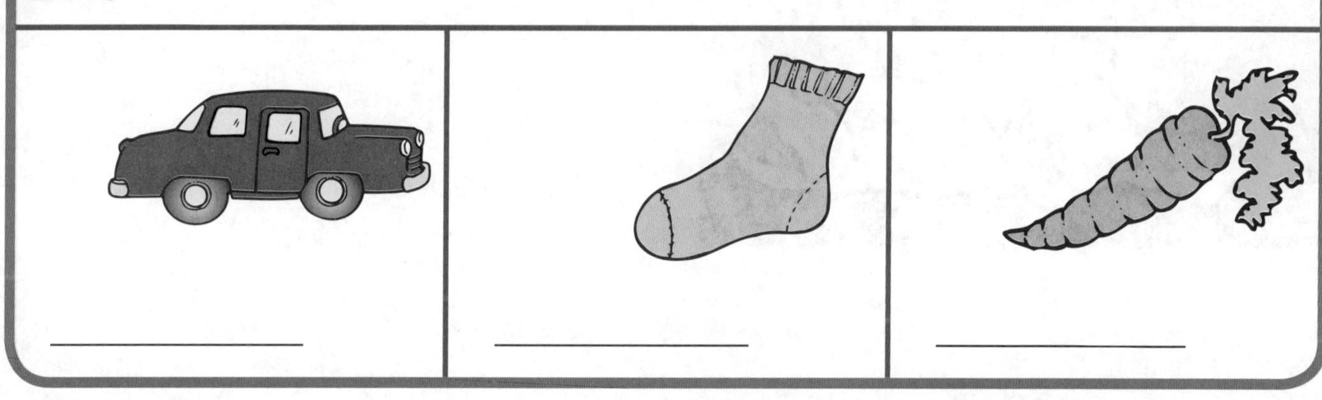

3.

Directions:

Initial Consonants (I-2): Review the sounds of **B** and **C**. Have students name the pictures. Ask them to write **B** (for question I) and **C** (for question 2) below each picture whose name begins with that sound. Have students put an **X** directly on the picture that does not begin with that sound.

Sequence (3): Have students look at all three pictures. Ask them to write **I** below the event that would happen first, **2** below the event that would happen second, and **3** below the event that would happen third.

Max Plays

Max plays.

What is Max doing?

Max rolls over.

How do you think Max feels?

Max rolls over and over.

Max is happy.

What will Max do next?

Name ___________________________

1. D

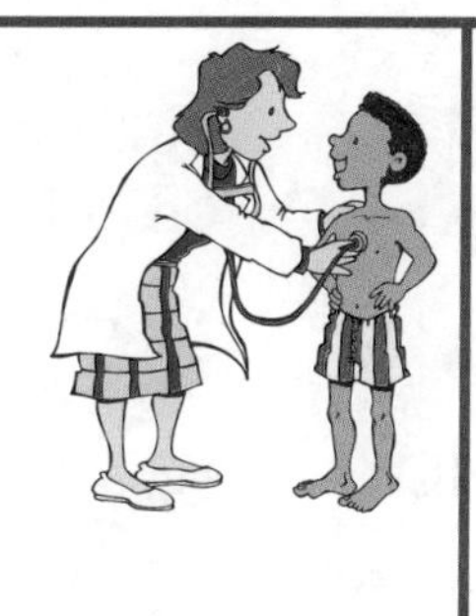
____

____

____

2. F

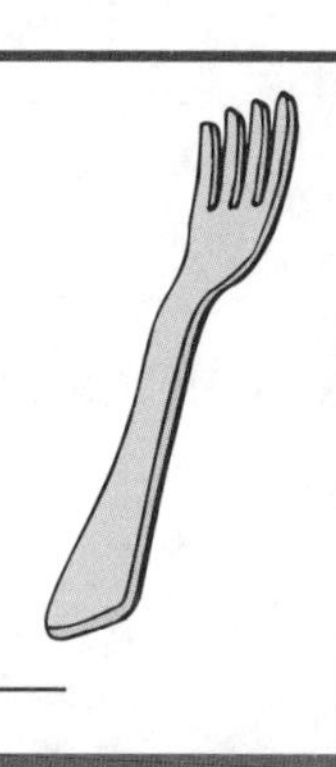
____

____

____

3.

See Max jump.

Here is Max.

4.

Max rolls over.

Max hides.

Directions:

Initial Consonants (1-2): Review the sounds of **D** and **F**. Have students name the pictures. Have them write **D** (for question 1) and **F** (for question 2) below each picture whose name begins with that sound. Ask students to put an **X** directly on the picture that does not begin with that sound.

Picture Clues (3-4): Ask students to read the sentences in each box and circle the sentence that best describes the picture.

Look, Max!

Look, Max.

What does Max see?

Look, Max, look.

Why is Max doing what he is doing?

Max wags his tail.

How do you think Max feels?

Max looks.

What do you think will happen next?

Name ______________________________

I. G

 ______	 ______	 ______

2. H

 ______	 ______	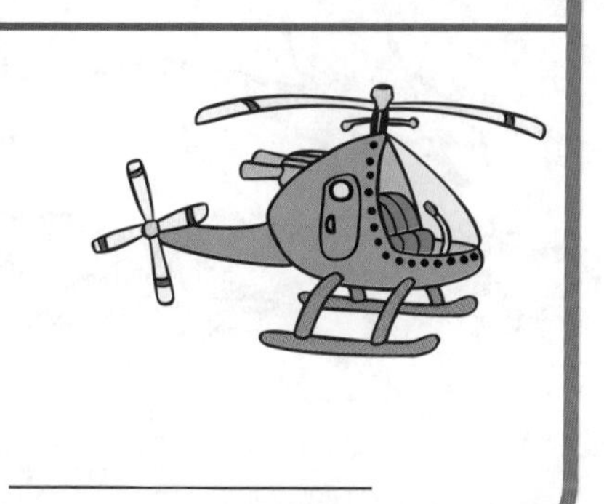 ______

3. Max looks.	yes	no
4. Max runs away.	yes	no
5. Max wags his tail.	yes	no
6. Max eats.	yes	no

Directions:
Initial Consonants (1-2): Review the sounds of **G** and **H**. Have students name the pictures. Have them write **G** (for question 1) and **H** (for question 2) below each picture whose name begins with that sound. Ask students to put an **X** directly on the picture that does not begin with that sound.
Facts and Details (3-6): Introduce the words *yes* and *no*. Ask students to read each sentence. Then, based on the story events, circle the correct answer.

Max Jumps

Max looks.

What does Max see?

Max jumps.

Max plays.

What is Max doing?

Jump, Max!

What should Max do?

Name ______________________________

1. J

2. K

3.

Max goes in.

Max goes out.

4.

Max finds the ball.

Max lost the ball.

Directions:

Initial Consonants (1-2): Review the sounds of **J** and **K**. Have students name the pictures. Have them write **J** (for question 1) and **K** (for question 2) below each picture whose name begins with that sound. Ask students to put an **X** directly on the picture that does not begin with that sound.

Picture Clues (3-4): Ask students to read the sentences in each box and circle the sentence that best describes the picture.

Max Meets Max

Max looks.

It looks.

What does Max see? What is he looking into?

Max sits up.

It sits up.

What does Max think he sees?

Max jumps.

It jumps up.

How does Max feel about what he sees?

Max wags his tail.

It wags its tail.

How many tails are really wagging?

Name ____________________

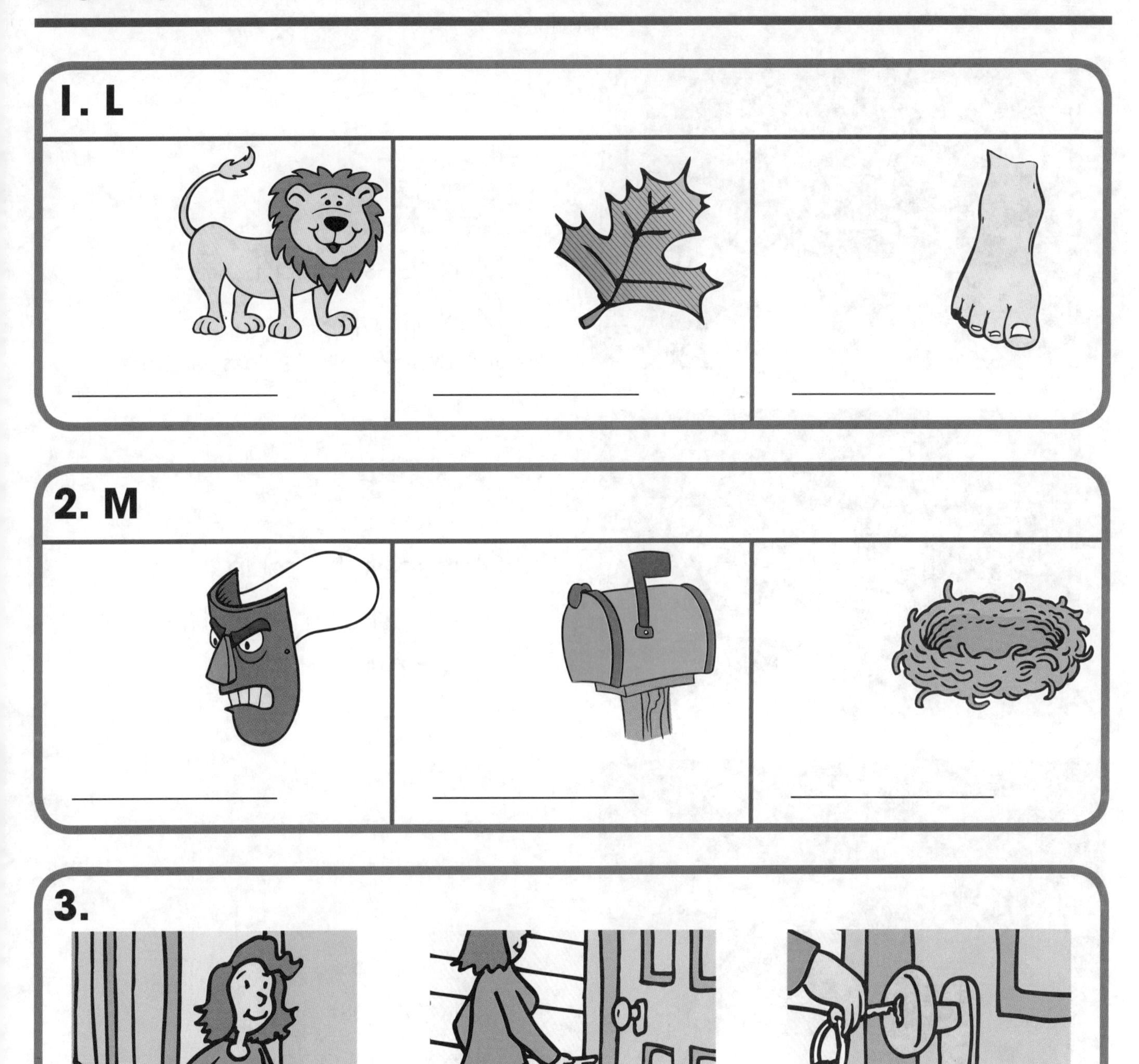

Directions:

Initial Consonants (1-2): Review the sounds of **L** and **M**. Have students name the pictures. Ask them to write **L** (for question 1) and **M** (for question 2) below each picture whose name begins with that sound. Have students put an **X** directly on the picture that does not begin with that sound.

Sequence (3): Have students look at all three pictures. Ask them to write **1** below the event that would happen first, **2** below the event that would happen second, and **3** below the event that would happen third.

Max Meets a Man

Max sees a man.

Max sits up.

What does Max see? Why does he sit up?

Max sees the man.

The man comes to the door.

Max barks.

Why do you think Max barks?

Max jumps.

Max barks again.

Max wags his tail.

The man smiles.

Why do you think Max wags his tail?

Name ______________________________

3. Max can ________ the ball.

jump

walk

get

4. Max can't ________ a book.

eat

read

look

Directions:
Initial Consonants (1-2): Review the sounds of **N** and **P**. Have students name the pictures. Have them write **N** (for question 1) and **P** (for question 2) below each picture whose name begins with that sound. Ask students to put an **X** directly on the picture that does not begin with that sound.
Context Clues (3-4): Ask students to read each sentence and circle the word that best completes the sentence.

Max Digs a Hole

Max sees an animal.

What kind of animal has Max found? Where do you think the animal came from?

The rabbit runs into a hole.

Can the rabbit play?

What does Max want the rabbit to do?

Max digs a bigger hole.

What is Max doing now?

Max is tired.

Why did Max stop digging?

Name ____________________

1. R

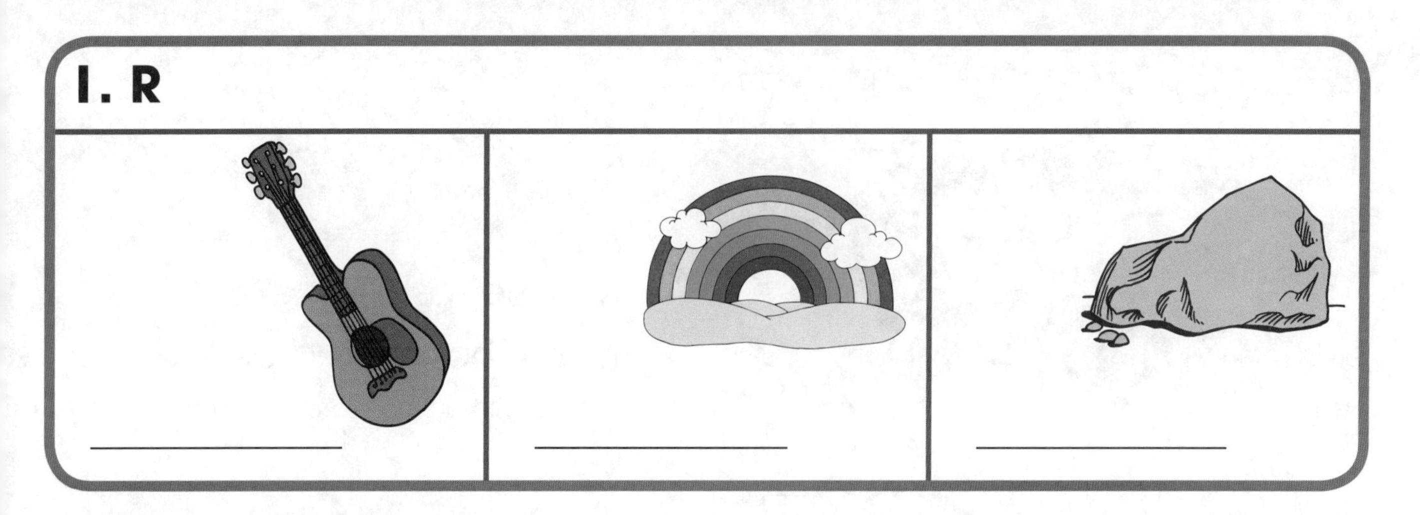

2. S

3.

Directions:

Initial Consonants (1-2): Review the sounds of **R** and **S**. Have students name the pictures. Ask them to write **R** (for question 1) and **S** (for question 2) below each picture whose name begins with that sound. Have students put an **X** directly on the picture that does not begin with that sound.

Sequence (3): Have students look at all three pictures. Ask them to write **1** below the event that would happen first, **2** below the event that would happen second, and **3** below the event that would happen third.

Dreamy Max

Max sleeps.

Max is having a dream.

What do you think Max is dreaming about?

Max dreams about food.

Max smiles.

Why do you think Max smiles?

Max licks his lips.

Max wags his tail.

What color is Max's tongue? What kind of food do you like?

A boy pets Max.

Max wakes up.

The boy gives Max a bone.

How do you think Max feels about what he sees? Did Max's dream come true?

Name ____________________

Directions:

Initial Consonants (1-2): Review the sounds of **T** and **V**. Have students name the pictures. Have them write **T** (for question 1) and **V** (for question 2) below each picture whose name begins with that sound. Ask students to put an **X** directly on the picture that does not begin with that sound.

Picture Clues (3-4): Ask students to read the sentences in each box and circle the sentence that best describes the picture.

Max Sees Snow

Max sees white things.

What is happening?

Max sees snow falling.

What does Max see? What should Max do?

Come back, Max!

Why is Max running? Where should he go?

Max comes home.

Sleep, Max, sleep.

Why is Max tired? How does Max feel now?

Name ____________________

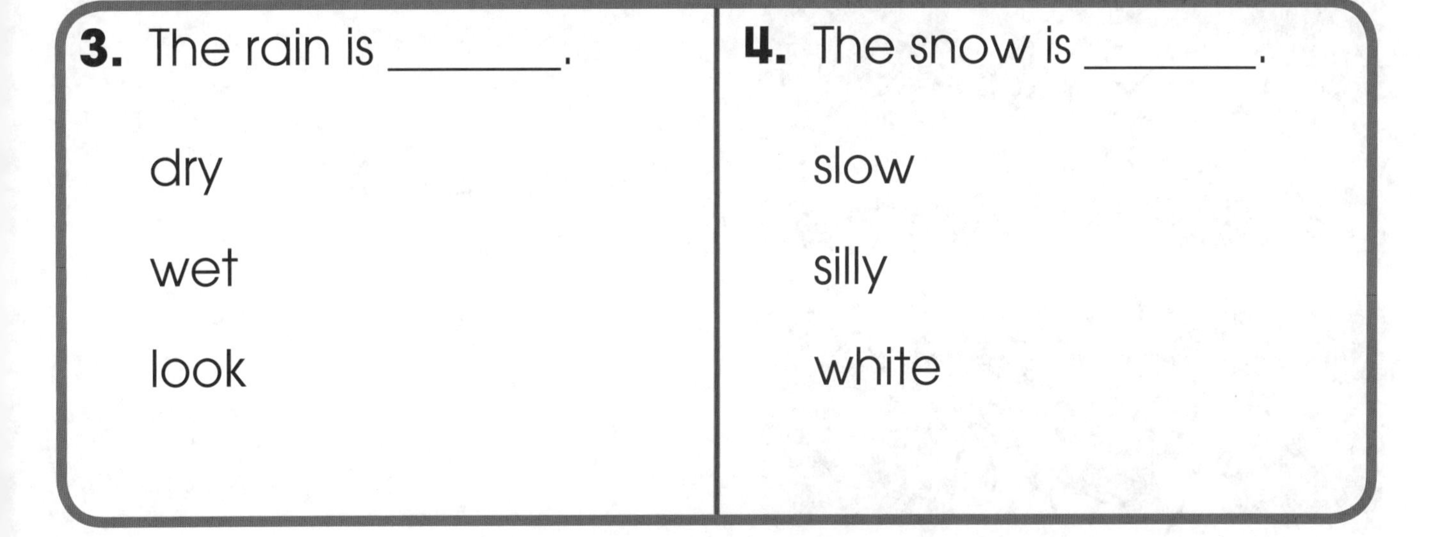

Directions:
Initial Consonants (1-2): Review the sounds of **W** and **Y**. Have students name the pictures. Have them write **W** (for question 1) and **Y** (for question 2) below each picture whose name begins with that sound. Ask students to put an **X** directly on the picture that does not begin with that sound.
Context Clues (3-4): Ask students to read each sentence and circle the word that best completes the sentence.

Dizzy Max

Max sees a bird.

He wants to play.

Where is the bird?

Max runs after the bird.

Max runs and runs.

How do you think Max feels?

The bird flies away.

What did the illustrator of this story do?

Max is dizzy.

What happened to Max? What should Max do now?

Name

3. Max does not want to play.	yes	no
4. Max feels tired.	yes	no
5. Max runs away from a rabbit.	yes	no
6. Max can't find the bird.	yes	no

Directions:

Initial Consonants (1): Review the sound of **Z**. Have students name the pictures. Have them write **Z** below each picture whose name begins with that sound. Ask students to put an **X** directly on the picture that does not begin with that sound.

Final Consonants (2): Review the sound of the letter **R**. Ask students to name each picture. Direct them to write **R** below each picture whose name ends with the **R** sound. Have them put an **X** directly on the picture that does not end with the **R** sound.

Facts and Details (3-6): Review *yes* and *no*. Have students read each sentence. Then, based on the story events, have them circle the correct answer.

Max Looks

Max sees a hole.

Max looks inside.

It is dark.

What do you think Max sees?

Run, Max, run!

Why does Max run?

Max goes home.

How does Max feel?

Name ____________________

5. Max finds a ______.

bone

lamp

sled

6. Max ______ in the dirt.

rolls

slow

tall

Directions:

Final Consonants (1): Review the sound of the letter **T**. Have students name each picture. Direct them to write **T** below each picture whose name ends with the **T** sound. Ask students to put an **X** directly on the picture that does not end with the **T** sound.

Classification (2-4): Have students look at all four pictures in each row and then circle the three that belong together.

Drawing Conclusions (5-6): Ask students to read the sentences in each box. Then, have them circle the word that makes the most sense.

Max Sees a Cat

Max sees a cat.

The cat is fat.

The cat sits.

Who does Max see?

Max walks to the cat.

Max smiles.

The cat sits.

Is Max being friendly?

Max smiles again.

The cat sits.

Max sits.

The cat smiles back.

How does Max get the cat to smile back?

Name ______________________________

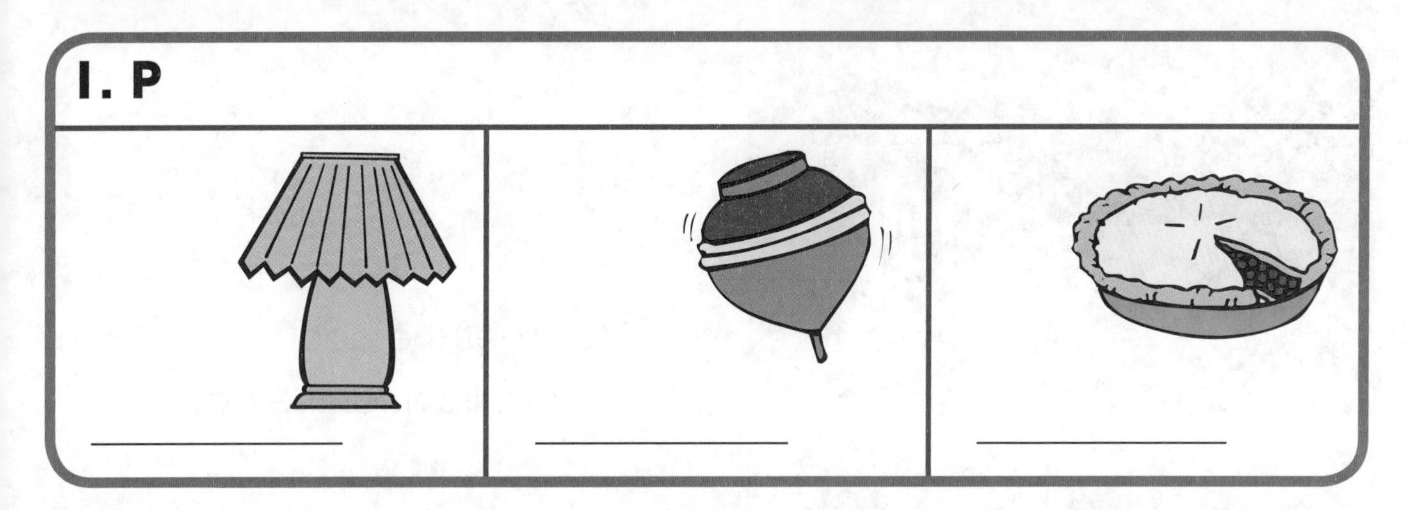

Directions:

Final Consonants (1): Review the sound of the letter **P**. Have students name each picture. Direct them to write **P** below each picture whose name ends with the **P** sound. Have students put an **X** directly on the picture that does not end with the **P** sound.

Short Vowels (2): Review the sound of short **A**. Have students name each picture. Direct them to write **A** below each picture whose name has the short-**A** sound. Ask them to put an **X** directly on the picture that does not have the short-**A** sound.

Max Takes a Splash!

Max sees the pool.

Max walks near the pool.

A boy is lying in the pool on a raft. Max walks to the edge of the pool. Max puts his nose in the water.

Why does Max put his nose in the water?

The boy says, "Come in, Max!" The boy waves his hand.

Why do you think the boy wants Max to come into the pool?

Max jumps into the pool and swims. The boy laughs.

Why does the boy laugh?

Name

Directions:

Final Consonants (1): Review the sound of the letter **L**. Have students name each picture. Direct them to write **L** below each picture whose name ends with the **L** sound. Have students put an **X** directly on the picture that does not end with the **L** sound.

Short Vowels (2): Review the sound of short **E**. Have students name each picture. Ask them to write **E** below each picture whose name has the short-**E** sound. Ask them to put an **X** directly on the picture that does not have the short-**E** sound.

Substituting Sounds (3-6): Have students read each word. Have them substitute the letter in boldface for the first letter of the word. Then, ask them to write the new word on the line.

Max Horses Around

Look, Max.

Max sees horses.

Max watches the horses jumping. Max wants to jump, too.

Why do you think Max wants to jump?

Max tries to jump over the fence. Max tries, but he falls.

What did the author of this story do?

The horses look at Max. They come closer. Max looks up at them.

Why do you think the horses stop jumping?

Name

1. N

2. K

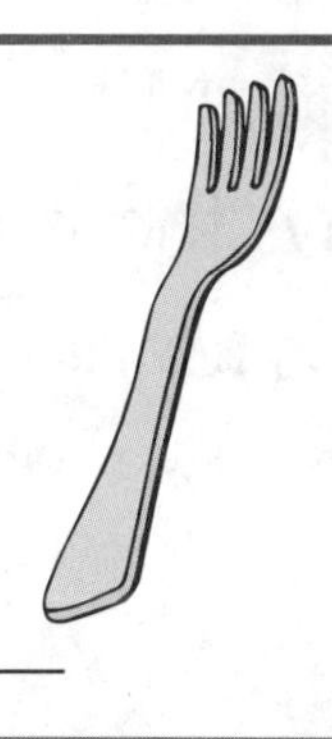

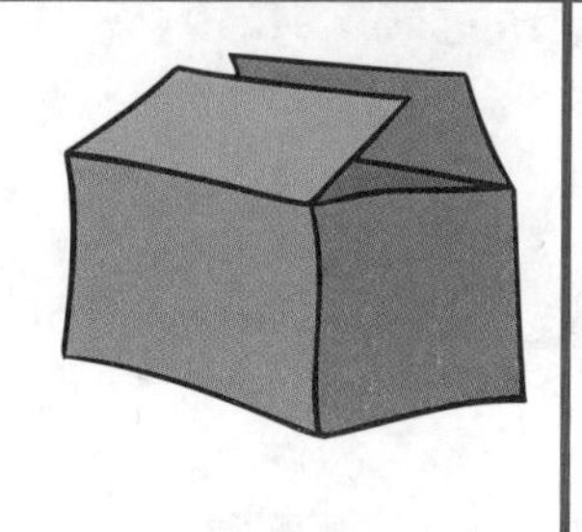

3. Max sees a toy.
He loves to play.
What will Max do?

Eat dinner
Play with the toy
Go to sleep

4. The cat wants to eat.
Food is in the house.
What will the cat do?

Stay outside
Go to sleep
Go inside the house

Directions:
Final Consonants (1-2): Review the sounds of the letters **N** and **K**. Have students name each picture. Direct them to write **N** (question 1) and **K** (question 2) below each picture whose name ends with that sound. Ask students to put an **X** directly on the picture that does not end with that sound.
Predicting Outcomes (3-4): Have students read the sentences at the top of each box. Then, have them circle the phrase below that makes sense.

The Big Race

Max gets into line.

Max looks at his friends.

What are Max and his friends going to do?

Get ready, Max.

"Go!" says the man.

Max starts running.

Do you think Max will win? Why or why not?

Max crosses the finish line.

He is first. He wins the race.

The crowd cheers.

Max gets a blue ribbon.

How do you think Max feels?

Name________________________________

1. S

2. I

6

3. Max _______ at his friends. winks smiles looks

4. Max _______ the race. loses wins forgets

5. Max crosses the finish line _______. last second first

6. "Go!" says the _______. man girl doggie

Directions:
Final Consonants (1): Review the sound of the letter **S**. Have students name each picture. Direct them to write **S** below each picture whose name ends with the **S** sound. Ask students to put an **X** directly on the picture that does not end with the **S** sound.
Short Vowels (2): Review the sound of short **I**. Have students name each picture. Ask them to write **I** below each picture whose name has the short-**I** sound. Have students put an **X** directly on the picture that does not have the short-**I** sound.
Facts and Details (3–6): Have students read each sentence. Then, based on story events, have them circle the correct answer.

The Birthday Dog

It is Max's birthday.

He is so happy.

Why are most people happy on their birthday?

Max walks into the yard.

He sees his friends.

Why are friends important?

They all shout, "Happy Birthday, Max! How old are you now?"

Max smiles.

He barks five times.

Why do you think Max barks five times?

Name ____________________

1. O

2. U

3. Max's friends have come over for his birthday party. What will they do?

sing
ski
take a nap

4. The cat forgot to bring a present. What will she do?

bring one tomorrow
run up a tree
hide under the table

Directions:
Short Vowels (1-2): Review the sounds of short **O** and short **U**. Have students name each picture. Direct them to write **O** (for question 1) and **U** (for question 2) below each picture whose name has that sound. Ask students to put an **X** directly on the picture that does not have that sound.
Predicting Outcomes (3-4): Have students read the sentences at the top of each box. Then, have them circle the phrase below that makes sense.

Hungry Max

Max is hungry.

Max looks around the kitchen for food.

Max looks at the bowls.

Max eats the cat's food.

Why do you think Max eats from the cat's bowl?

Max looks up.

He looks funny.

How do you think Max feels right now?

The cat comes in.

The cat looks at Max.

The cat smiles.

Why is the cat smiling?

Name

Directions:

Blends (1-2): Review the sounds of the blends **sn** and **pl**. Have students name each picture. Direct them to write **sn** (for question 1) and **pl** (for question 2) below each picture whose name begins with that sound. Ask students to put an **X** directly on the picture that does not begin with that sound.

Short Vowels (3-6): Have students name each picture and listen to the vowel sound. Ask them to circle the correct vowel below each picture.

Max and the Cat Play Catch

Max says hello to the cat.
They go outside.

Max and the cat find a ball.
They play catch.

Max throws the ball over the cat's head. The cat looks up at the ball.

What do you think will happen next?

The ball goes into the pool.
Max jumps into the pool.
The cat smiles.

Why does the cat smile?

Name____

1. sl

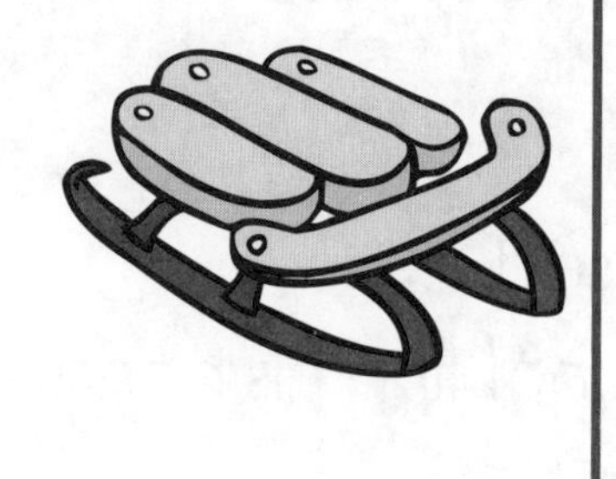

2. st

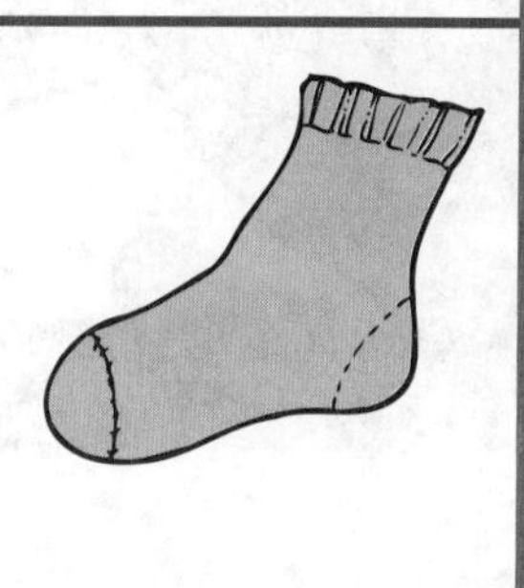

3. The cat and Max find a ball. Max throws it ________.

under
below
up

4. The cat and Max play catch. Max throws it ________ the cat's head.

over
under
on top of

Directions:

Blends (1-2): Review the sounds of the blends **sl** and **st**. Have students name each picture. Direct them to write **sl** (for question 1) and **st** (for question 2) below each picture whose name begins with that sound. Have students put an **X** directly on the picture that does not begin with that sound.

Predicting Outcomes (3-4): Have students read the sentences at the top of each box. Then, ask them to circle the word or phrase below that makes sense.

Max Is Sad

Max is sad.
He cannot find his bone.

Why is Max sad?

Max walks outside.
He lies down on the grass.

Max closes his eyes.
The cat comes outside.

Look at the picture. How do you think Max feels now?

The cat taps Max on the back. The cat gives Max a hug. Max feels better.

Why does Max feel better?

Name ______________________

1. tr

2.

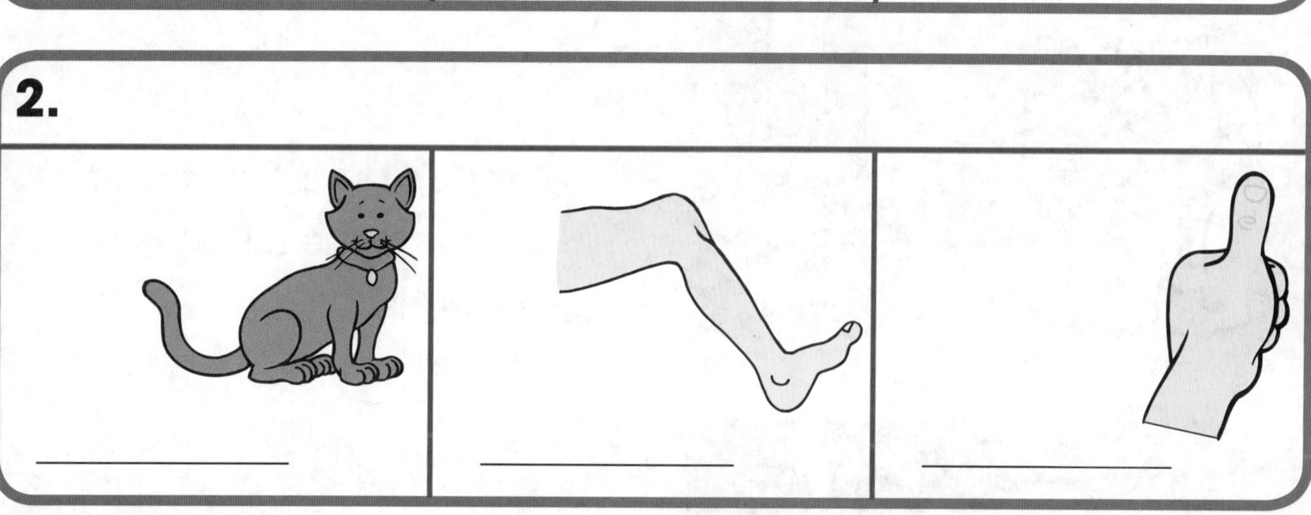

3. It is little.
It can make a web.
It has many legs.
What is it?

Ferris wheel
spider
caterpillar

4. It has four legs.
It is furry.
It says "Meow!"
What is it?

duck
cat
lamb

Directions:
Blends (1): Review the sound of the blend **tr**. Have students name each picture. Direct them to write **tr** below each picture whose name begins with the **tr** sound. Have students put an **X** directly on the picture that does not begin with the **tr** sound.
Short Vowels (2): Have students name each picture, listen to the vowel sound, and write the vowel below the picture.
Drawing Conclusions (3-4): Have students read the sentence riddles in each box. Then, have them circle the word that makes the most sense.

Max Goes to a Costume Party

Max is invited to a costume party. Max wants to wear a costume.

Max puts on a cat costume.

He looks in the mirror.

He laughs.

Why does Max laugh when he looks in the mirror?

Max walks to the costume party at a friend's house.

The cat opens the door.

Where is the costume party?

The cat is wearing a dog costume.

Max laughs. The cat laughs even harder.

What is funny about the way Max and the cat are dressed?

Name ____________________

1. fl

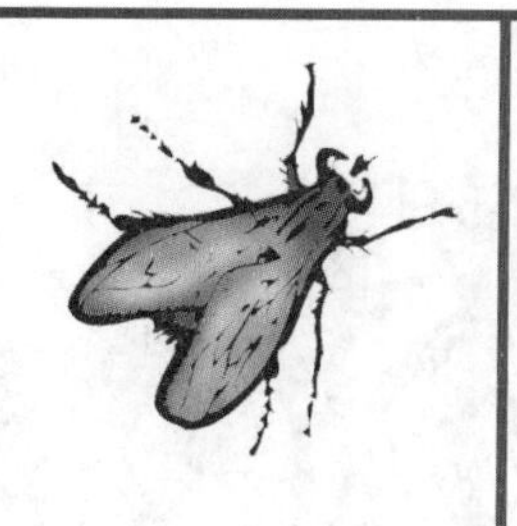
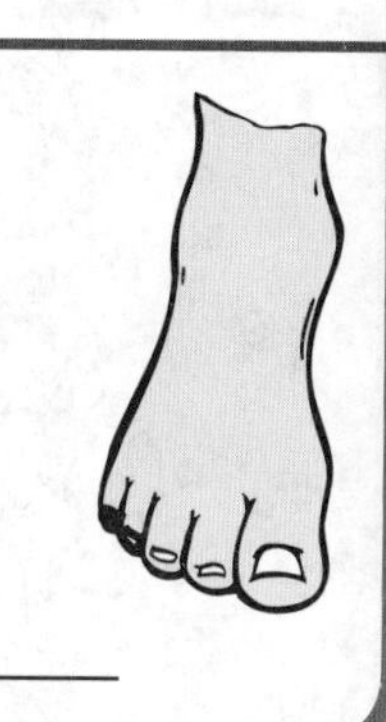

2.

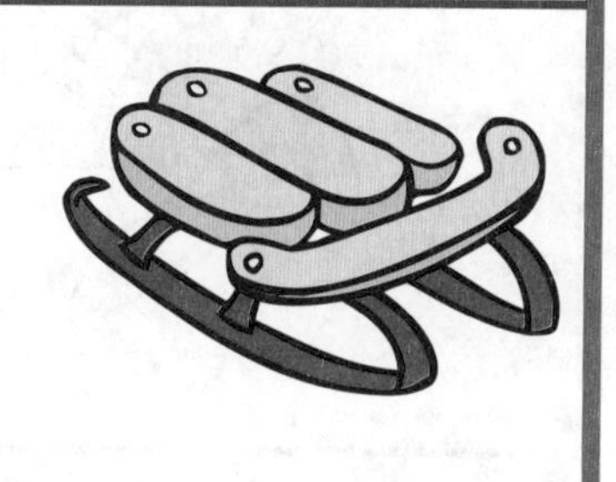

3. Max sees something. It jumps up from the water. Then, it jumps back in. *Splash*! What is it?

A bear
A frog
A tadpole

4. A squirrel runs down the tree and sees Max. Then, the squirrel runs up the tree. Where is the squirrel now?

The squirrel is with Max.
The squirrel is hiding in the leaves.

Directions:
Blends (1): Review the sound of the blend **fl**. Have students name each picture. Direct them to write **fl** below each picture whose name begins with the **fl** sound. Have students put an **X** directly on the picture that does not begin with the **fl** sound.
Blends (2): Have students name each picture, listen to the beginning sound, and write the blend below the picture.
Drawing Conclusions (3-4): Have students read the sentences at the top of each box. Then, ask them to circle the phrase or sentence below that makes the most sense.

Name

Same and Different

Directions:
Classification (1-4): Have students look at all four pictures in each row and circle the three that belong together.

Name

Sounds You Know

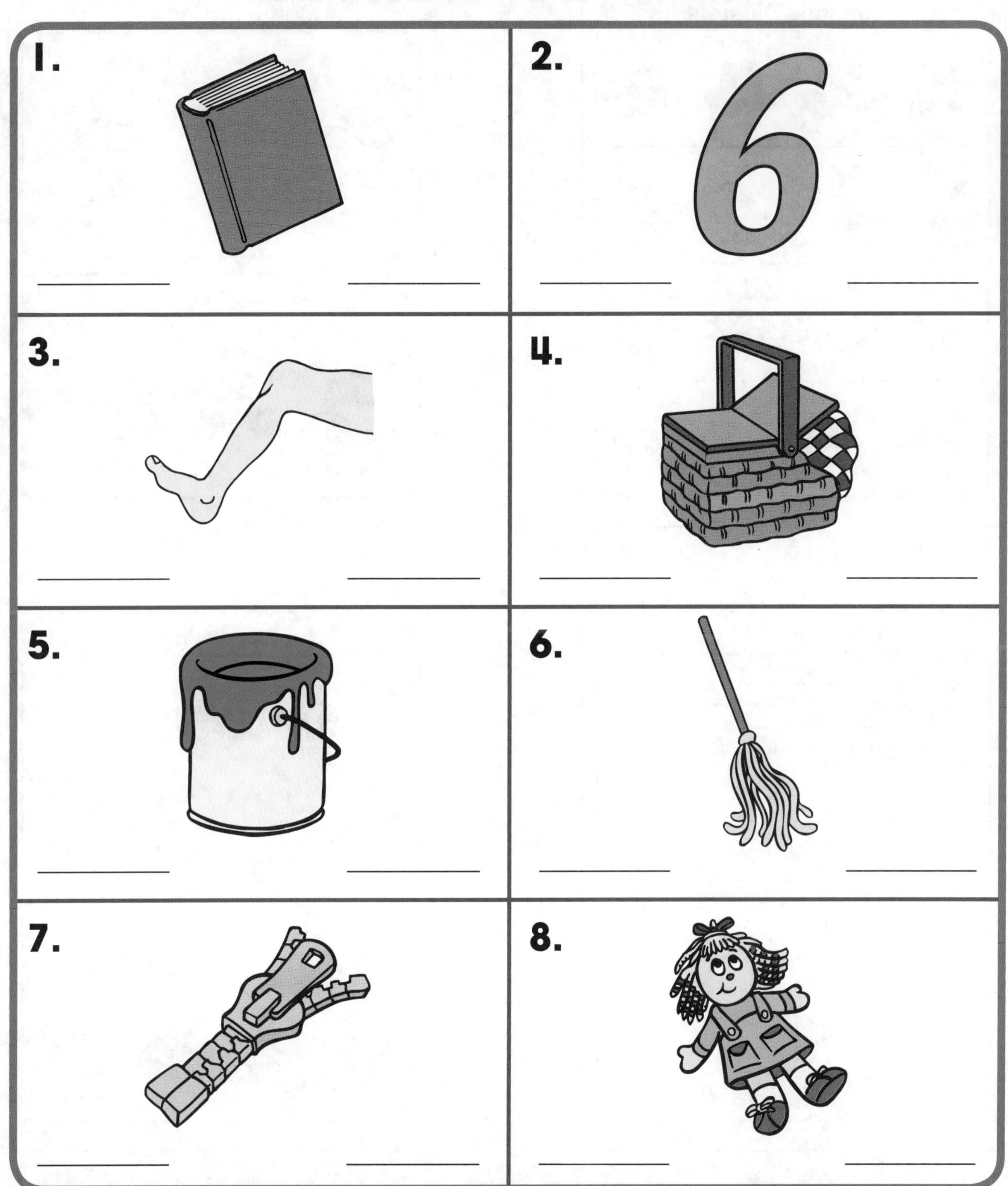

Directions:

Initial and Final Consonants (1-8): Have students look at each picture and say its name aloud. Have them listen to the beginning and ending consonants. Then, ask students to write down the beginning and ending consonants next to each picture.

Answer Key

3

Match the Picture

Matt blows a bubble with his gum.

Tia and Erik painted a rainbow together.

5

6

7

Answer Key

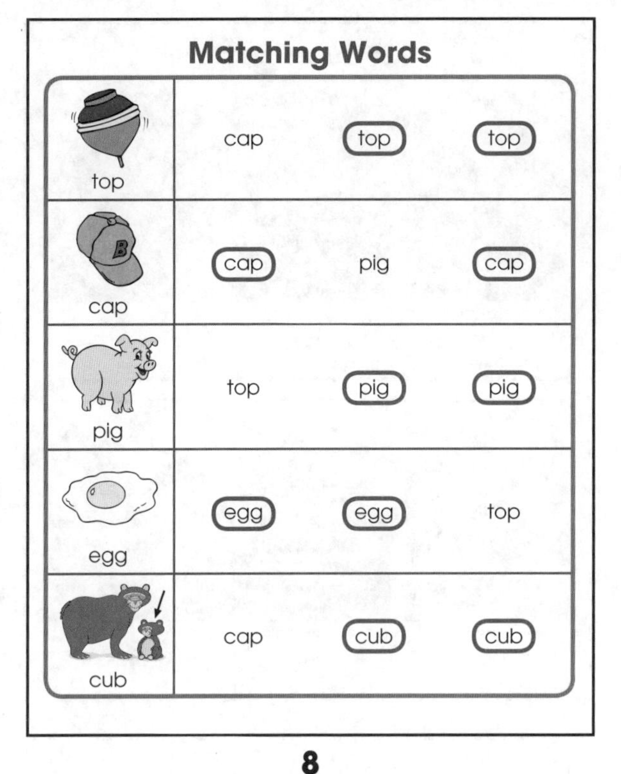

8

Matching Words

do	(do)	you	(do)
you	the	(you)	do
smell	do	(smell)	(smell)
the	(the)	you	(the)
cake	(cake)	smell	(cake)

9

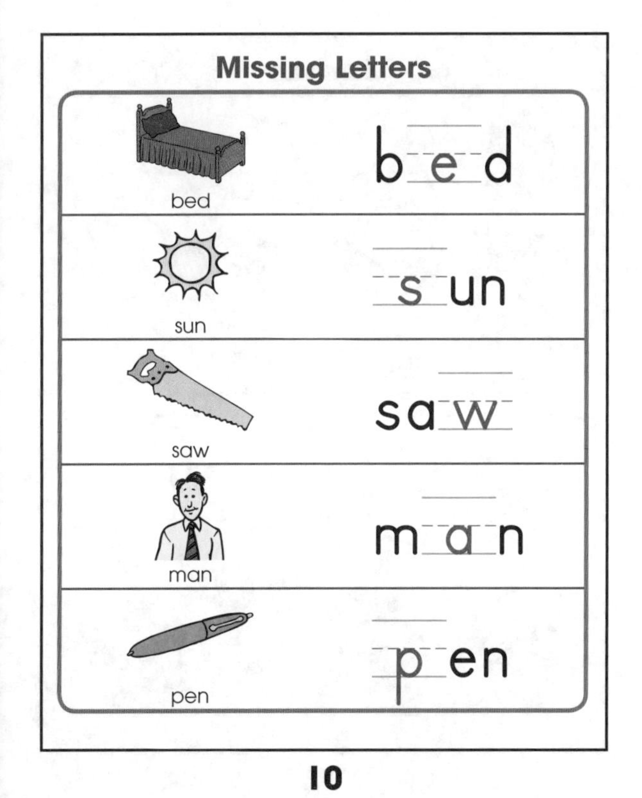

10

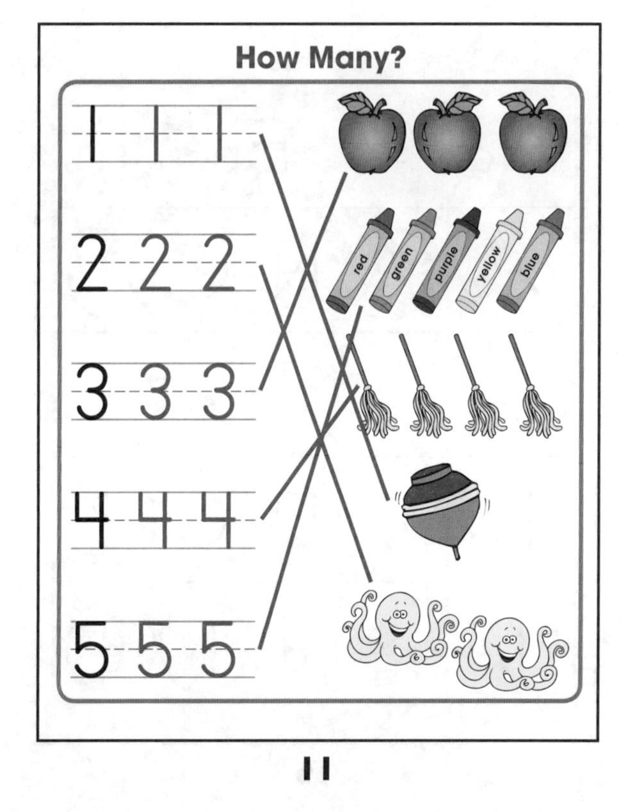

11

Answer Key

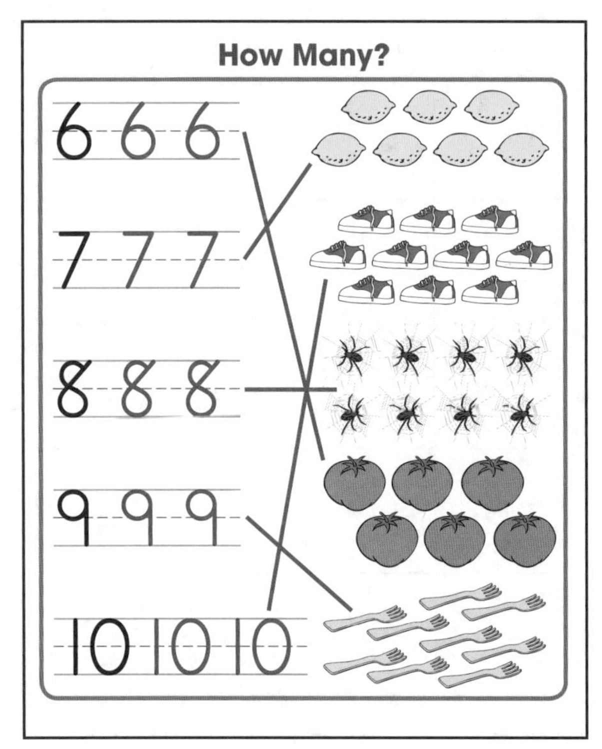

12

14

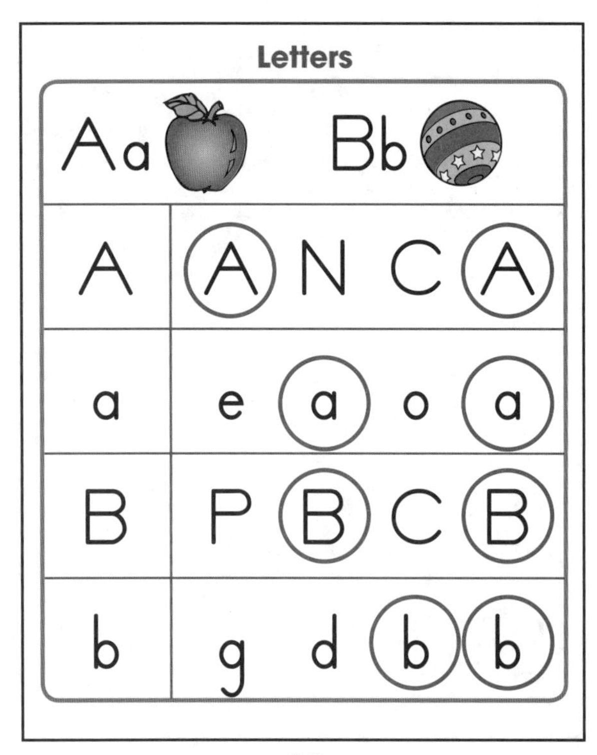

15

16

Answer Key

17

18

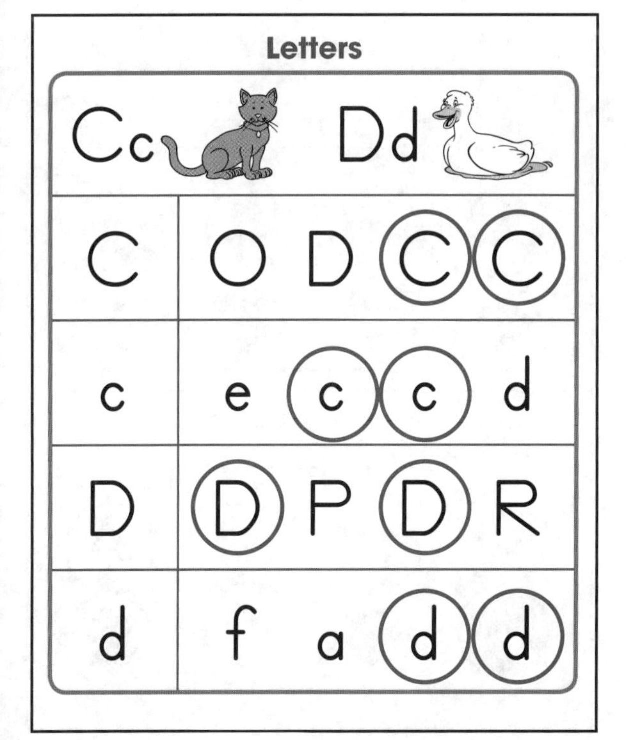

20

21

Answer Key

22

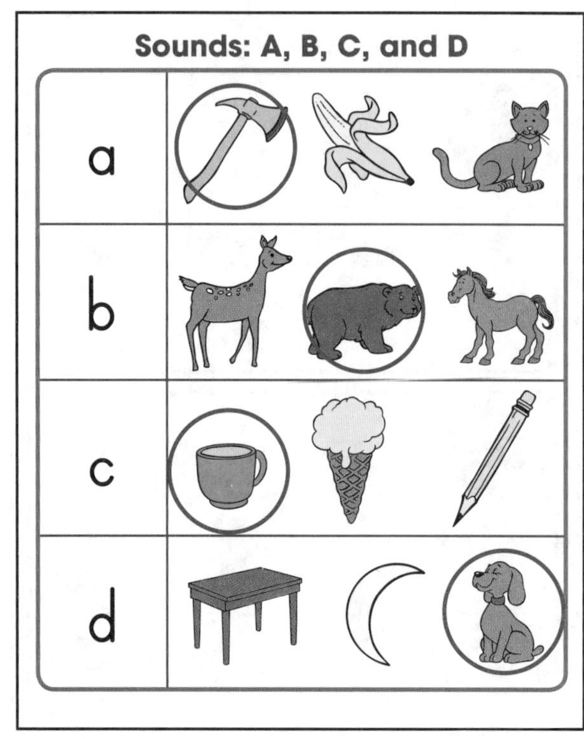

23

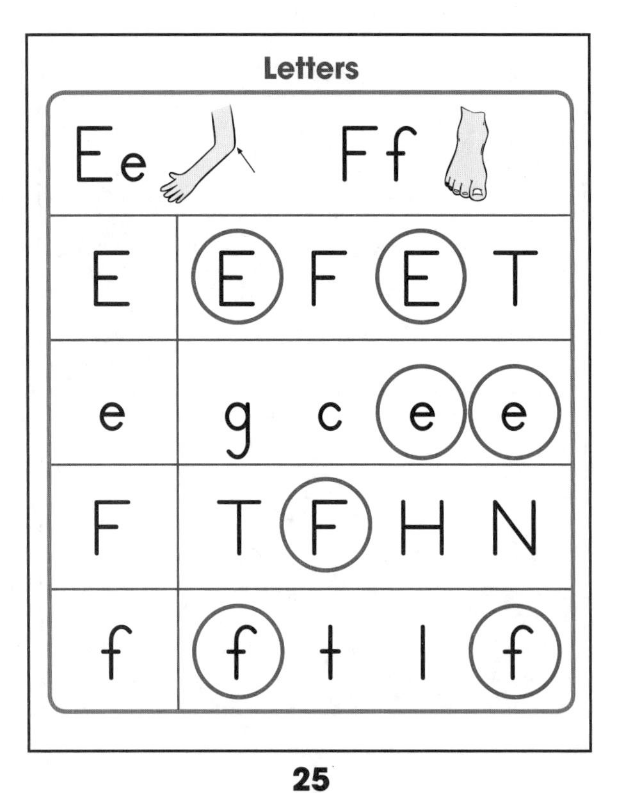

25

26

Answer Key

28

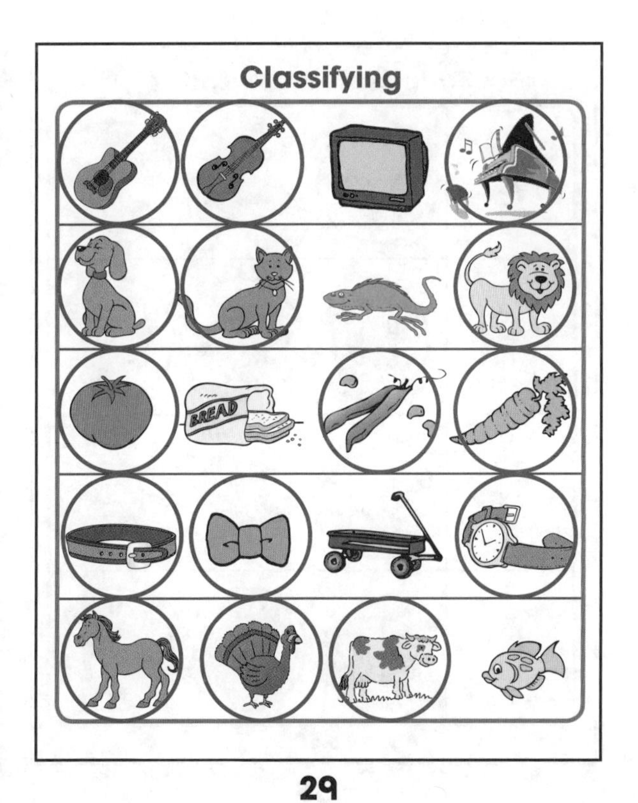

29

31

Answer Key

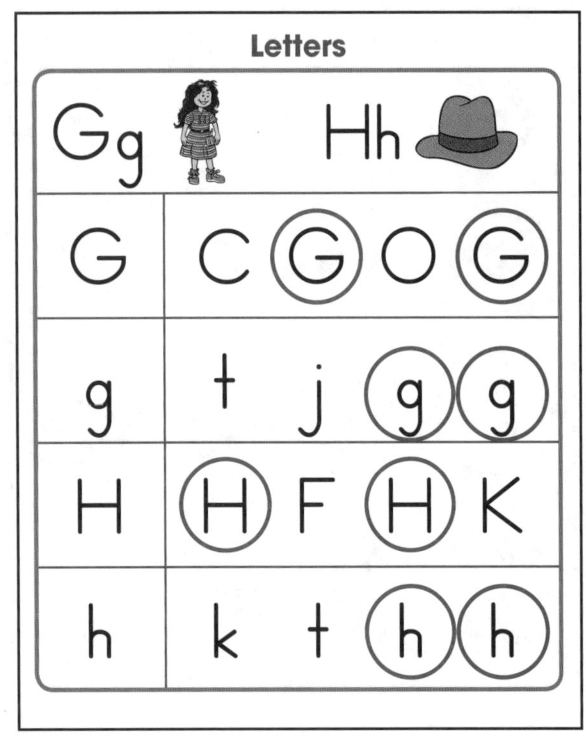

32

33

34

35

Answer Key

37

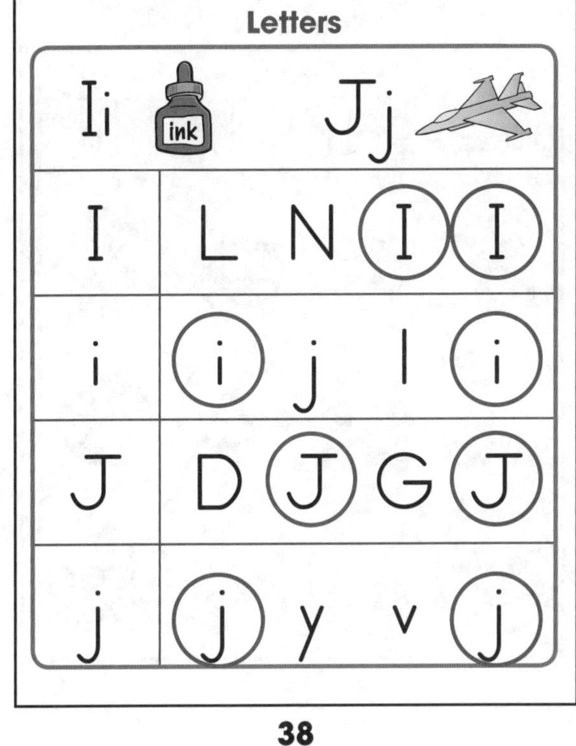

38

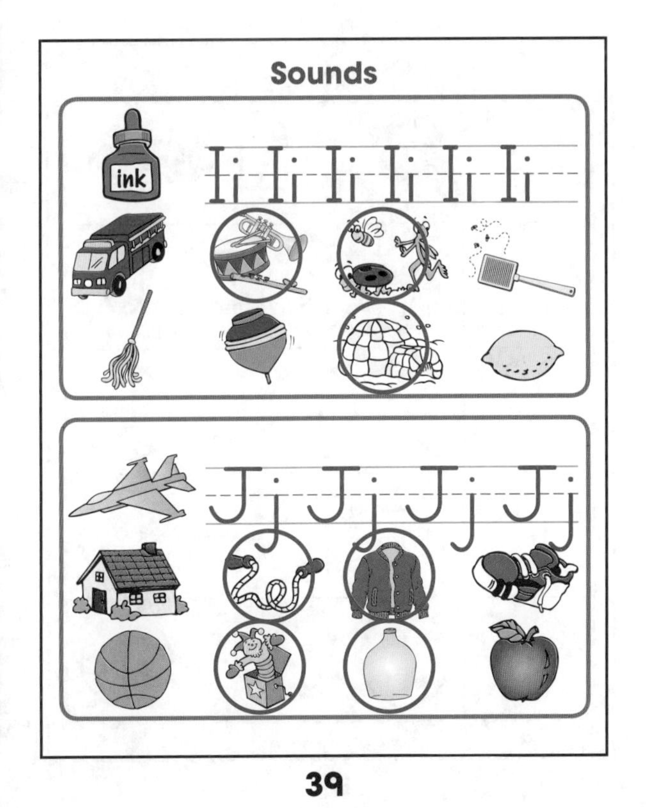

39

40

Answer Key

41

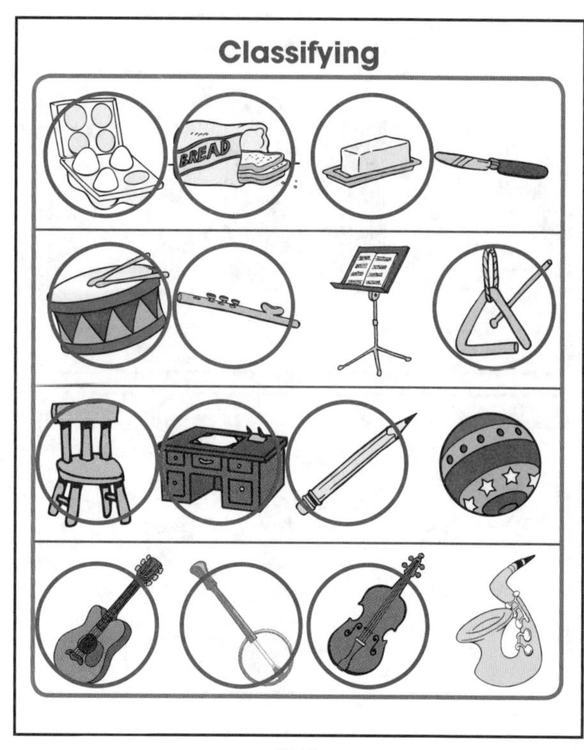

42

44

45

Answer Key

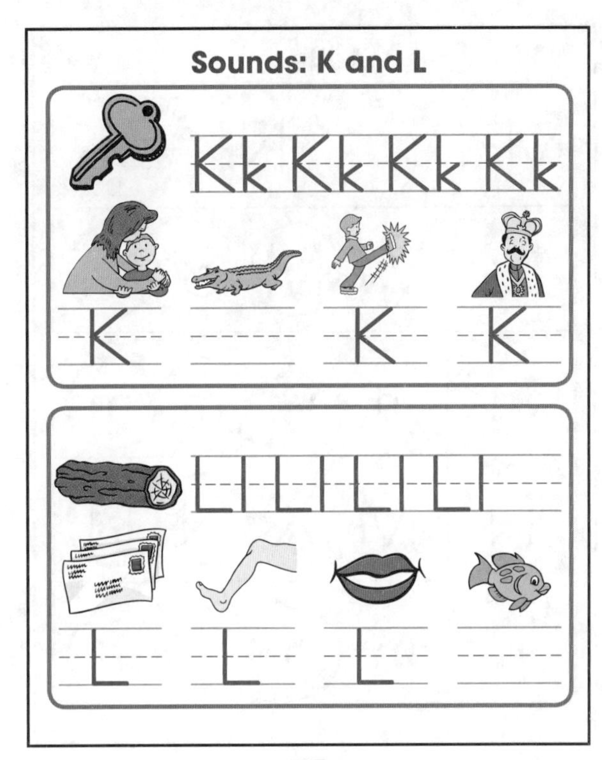

47

50

Answer Key

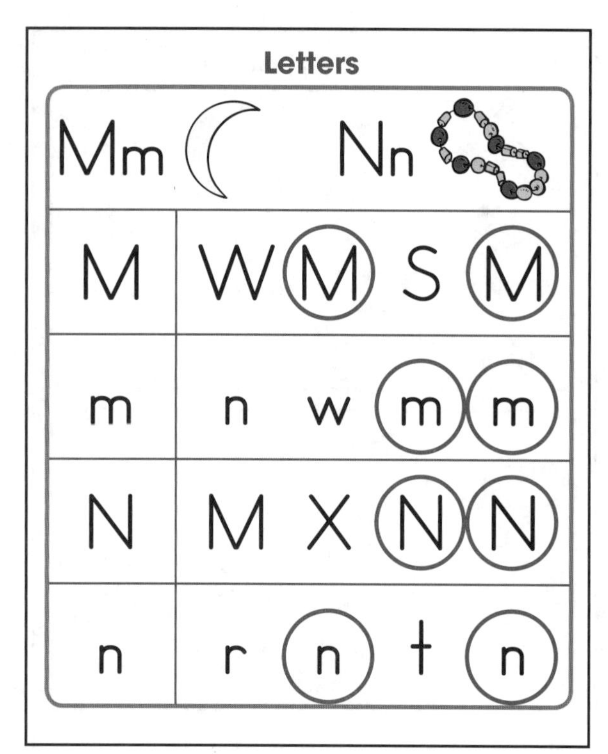

51

52

53

54

Answer Key

56

57

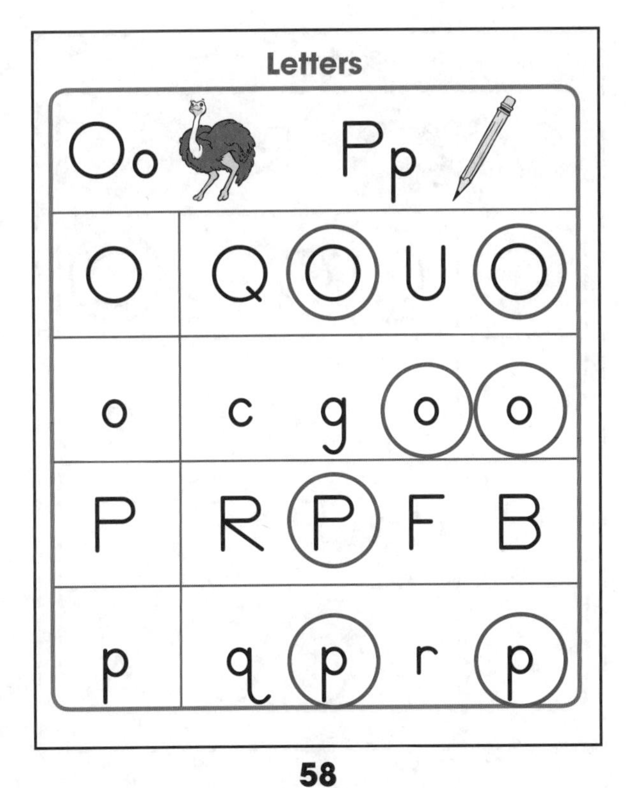

58

59

Answer Key

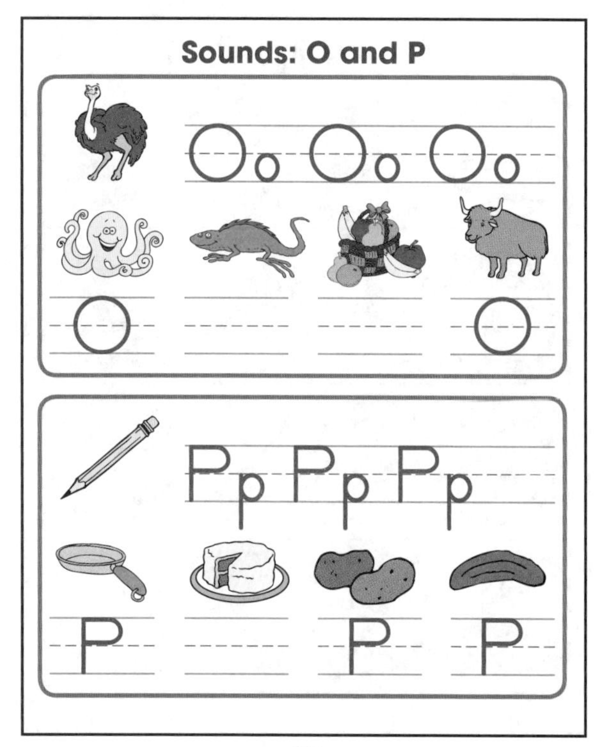

60

Sounds: O

Oo Oo Oo

61

62

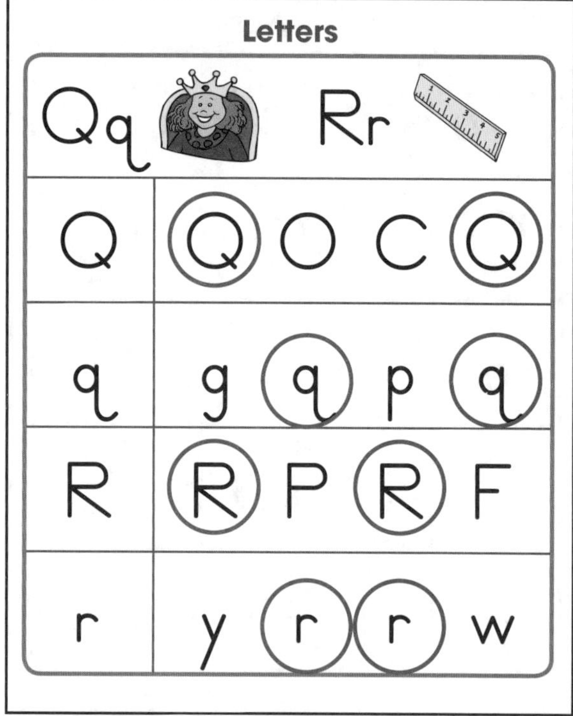

64

Answer Key

65

66

67

69

Answer Key

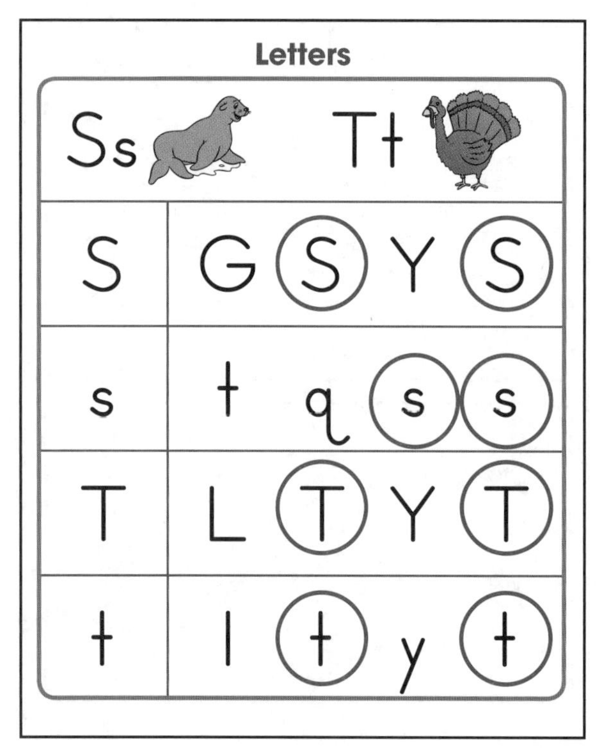

70

Sounds

Ss Ss Ss

SOAP

Tt Tt Tt

10

71

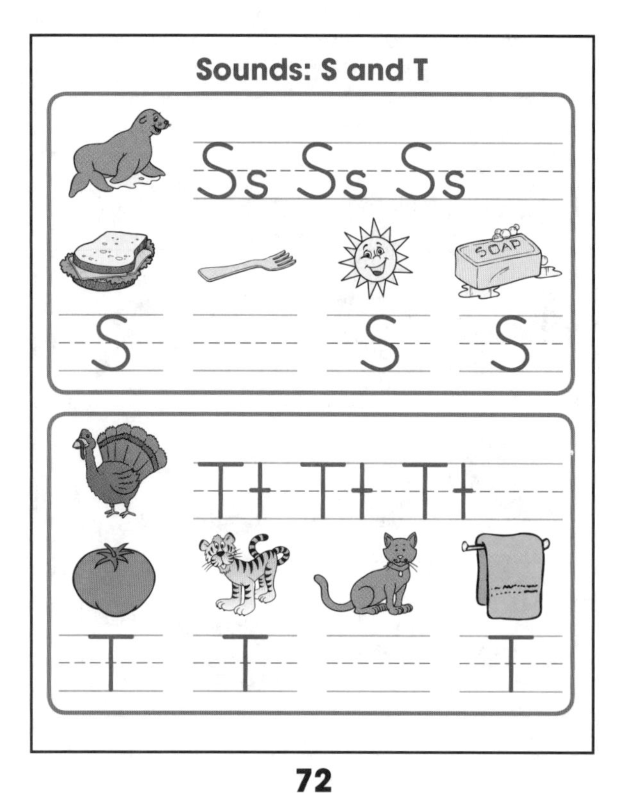

72

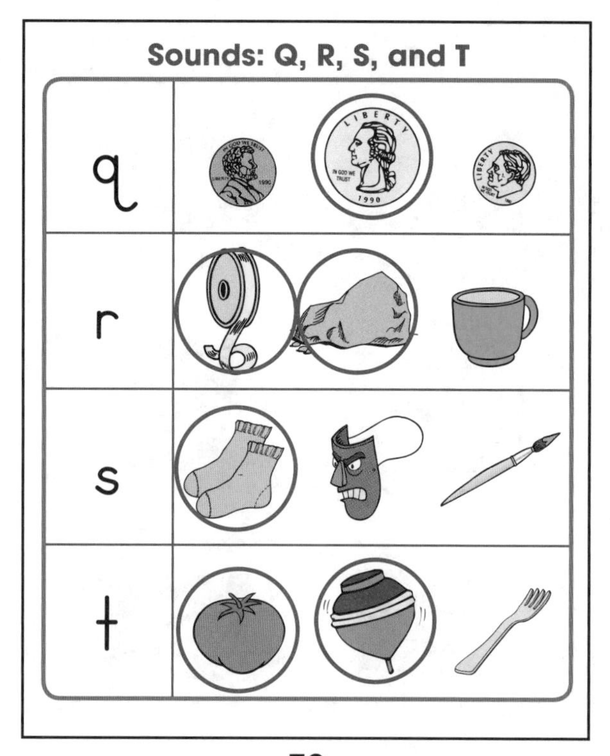

73

Answer Key

75

Letters

Uu Vv

U	V	(U)	W	(U)
u	(u)	n	(u)	v
V	Y	W	(V)	(V)
v	a	(v)	u	w

76

77

78

Answer Key

79

80

82

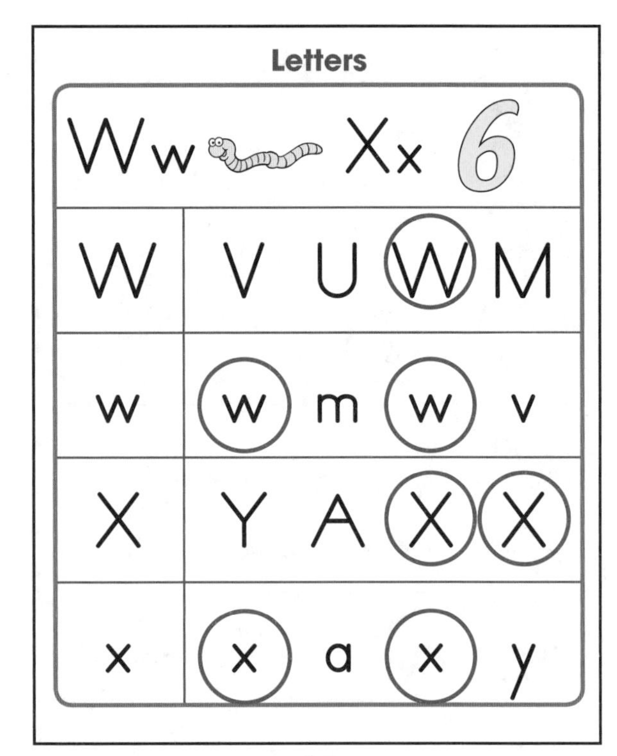

83

Answer Key

84

85

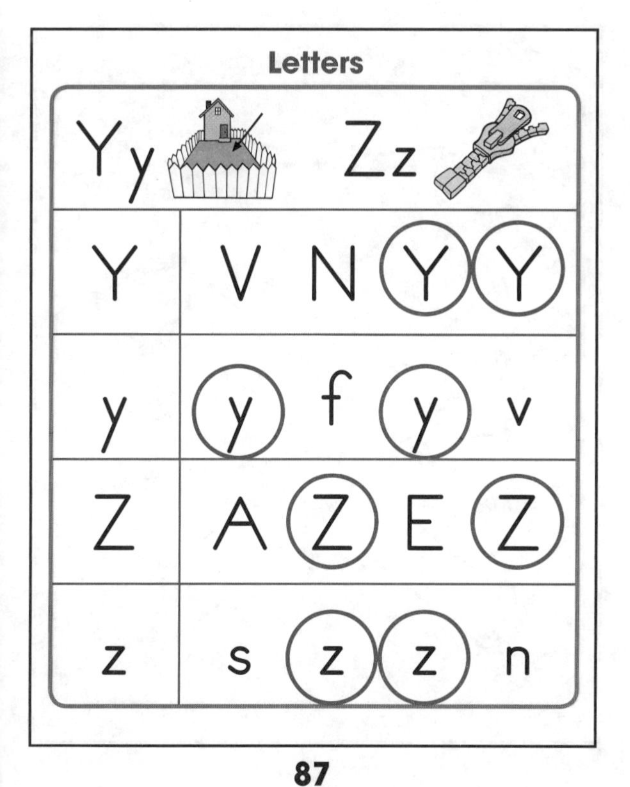

87

88

Answer Key

89

90

91

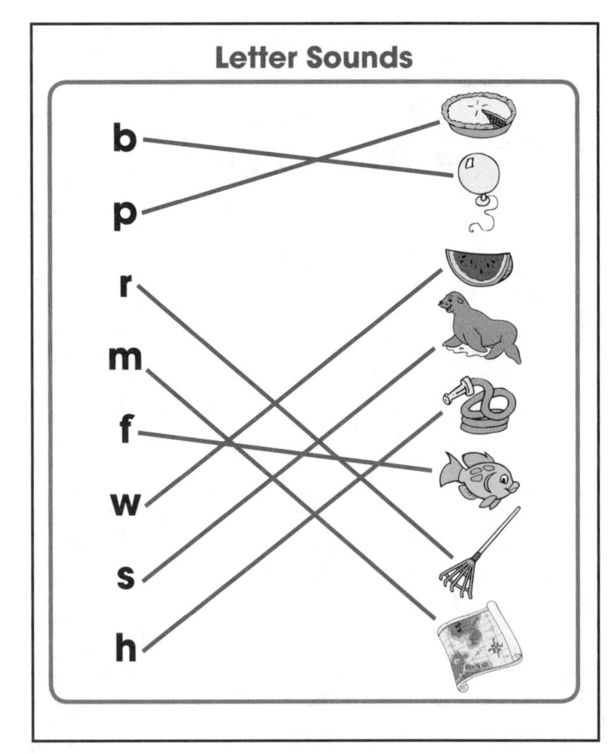

92

Answer Key

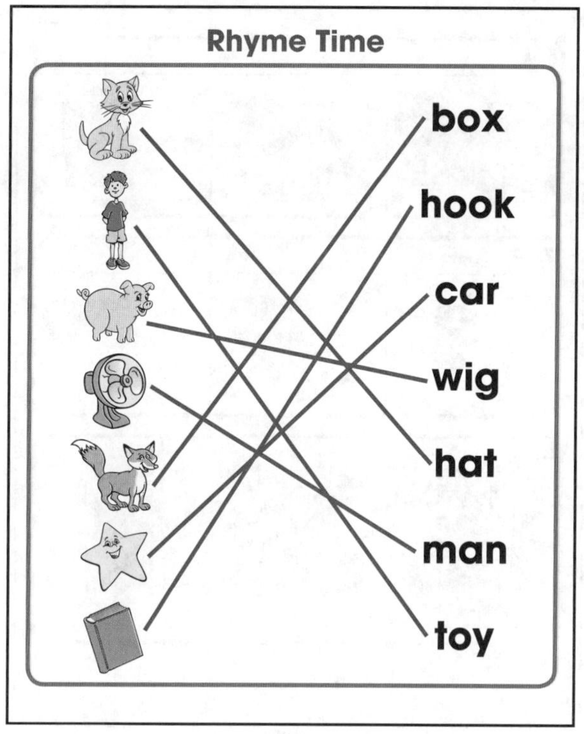

93

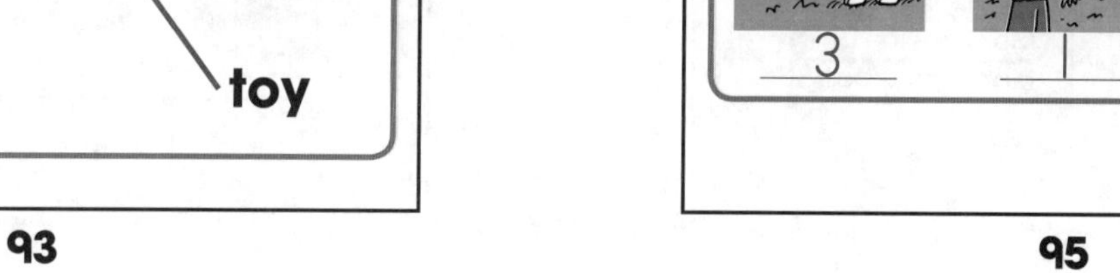

95

97

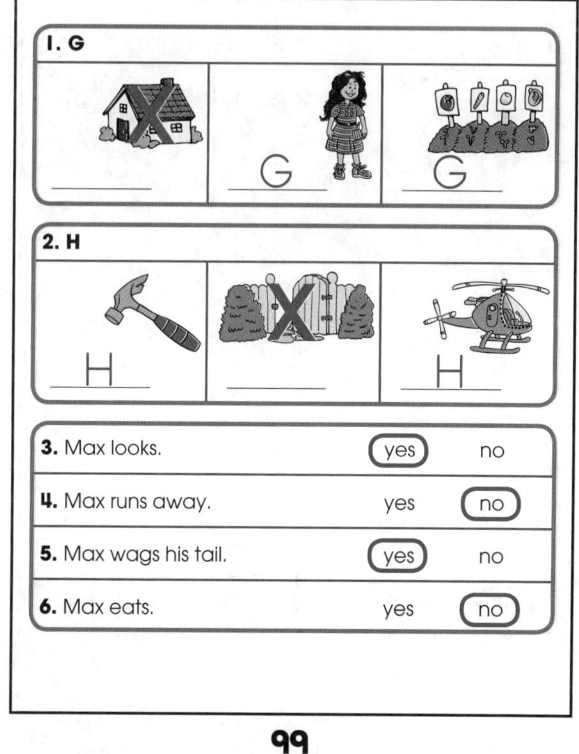

99

Answer Key

101

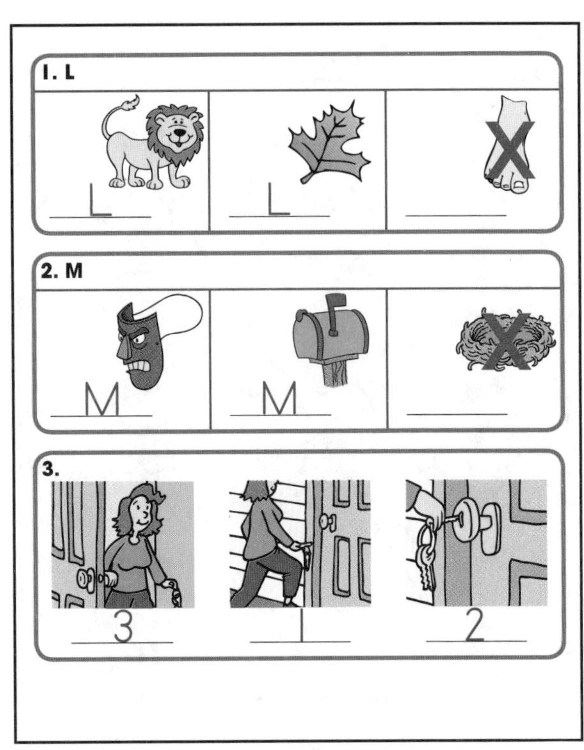

103

105

107

Answer Key

109

111

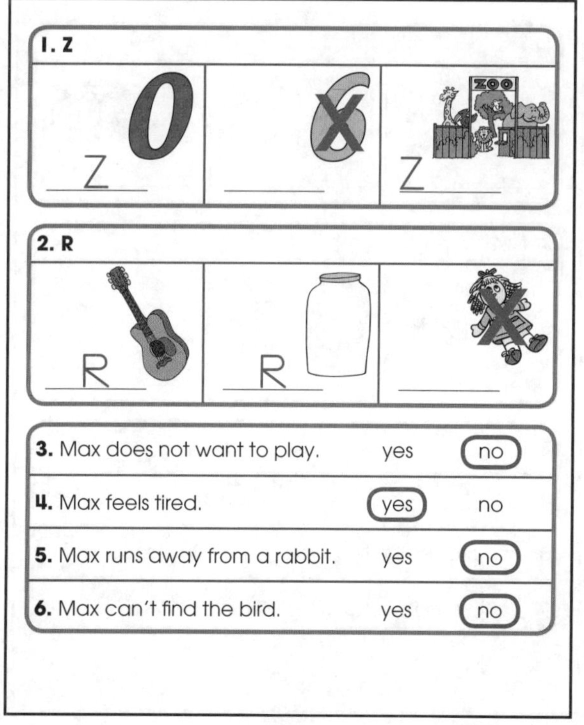

113

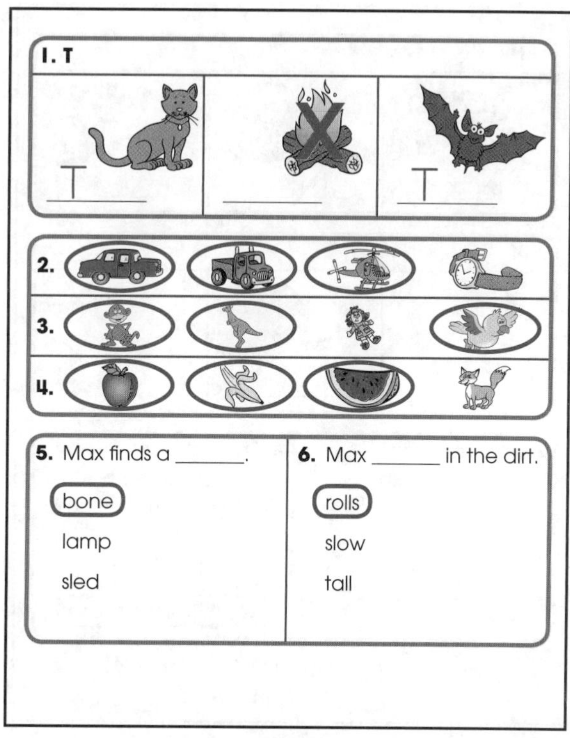

115

Answer Key

117

119

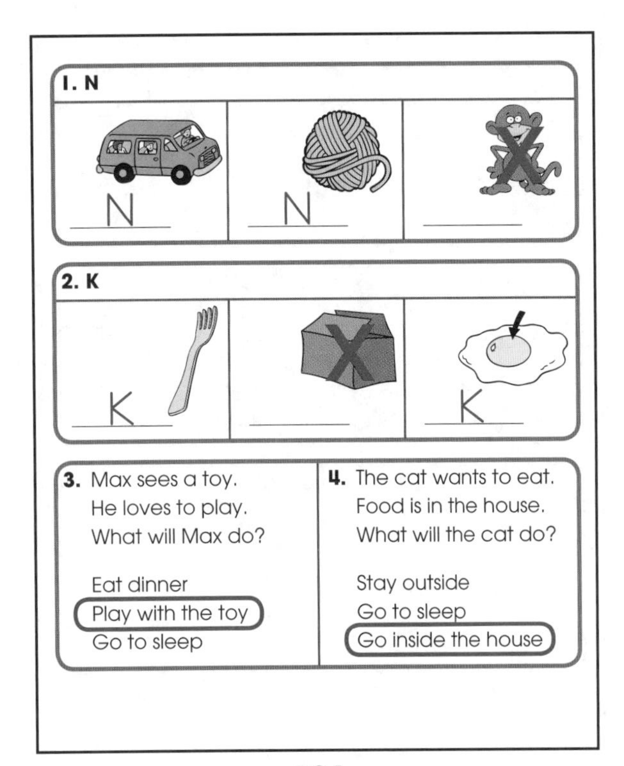

121

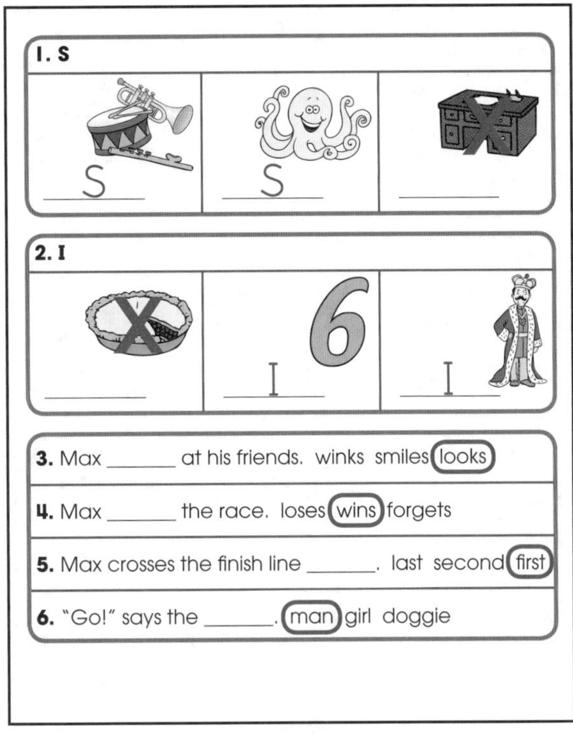

123

Answer Key

125

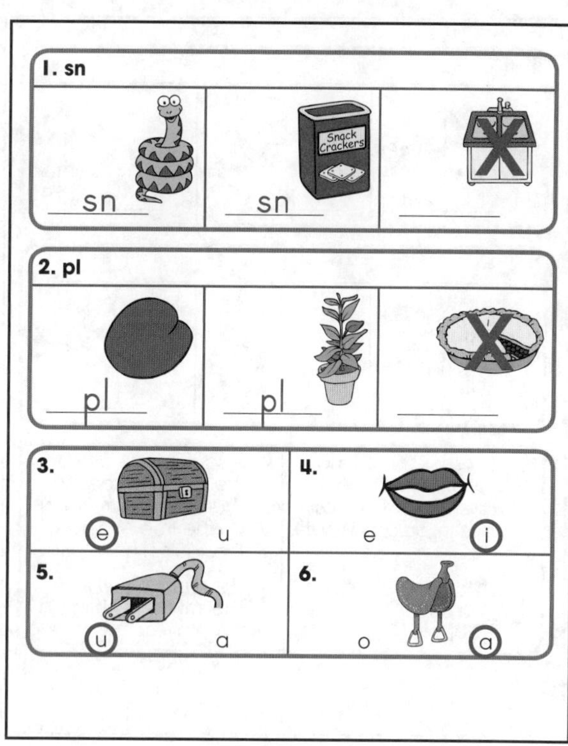

127

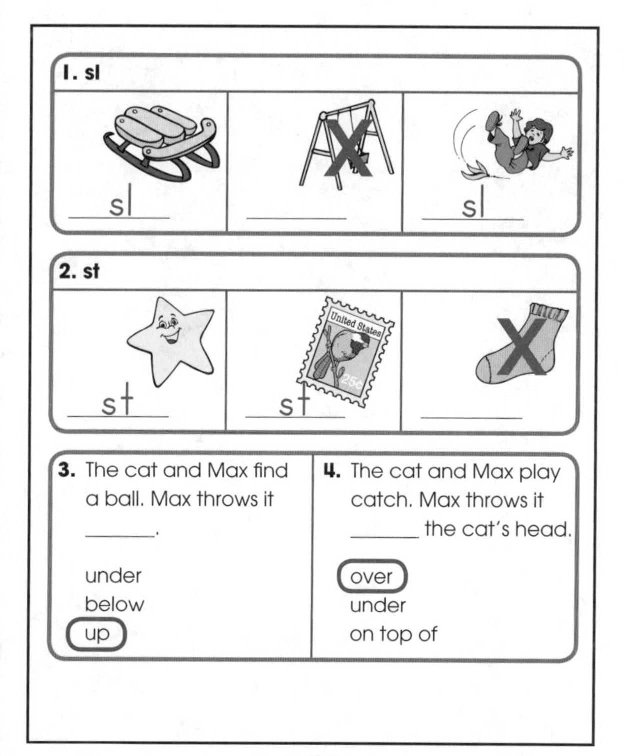

129

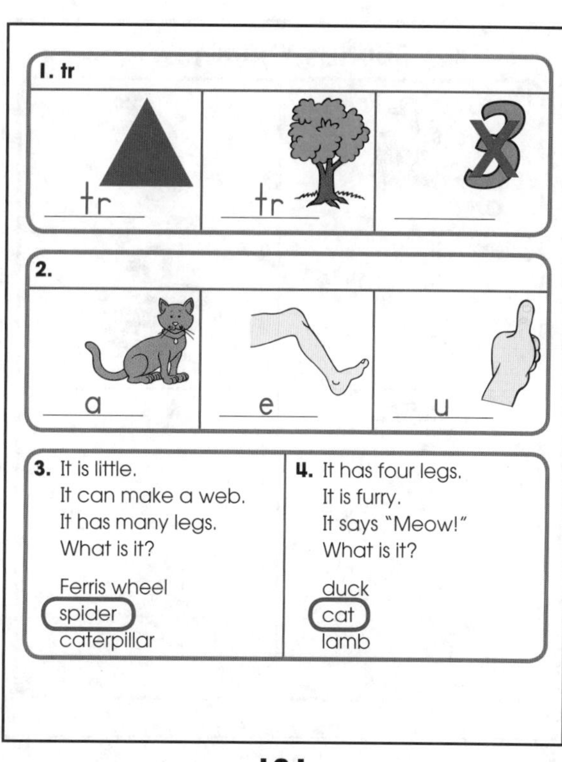

131

Answer Key

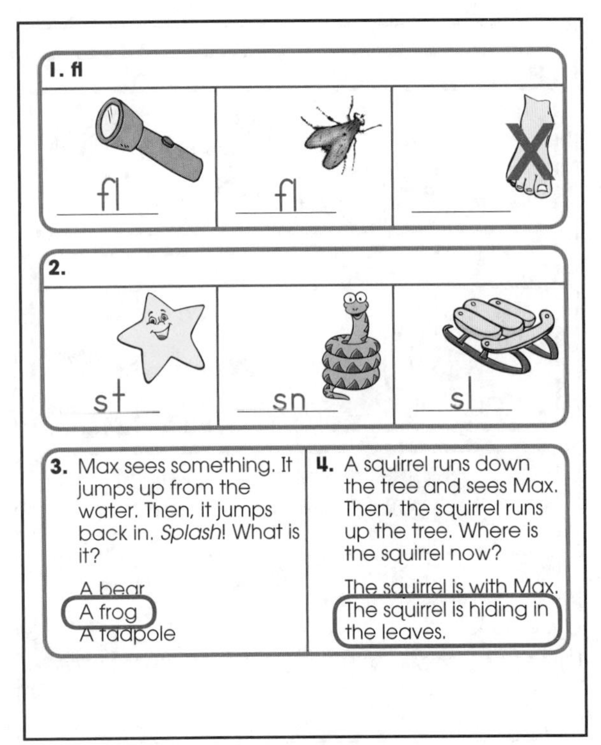
1. fl

fl fl

2.

st sn sl

3. Max sees something. It jumps up from the water. Then, it jumps back in. *Splash*! What is it?

A bear
A frog
A tadpole

4. A squirrel runs down the tree and sees Max. Then, the squirrel runs up the tree. Where is the squirrel now?

The squirrel is with Max.
The squirrel is hiding in the leaves.

133

Same and Different

1.

2.

3.

4.

134

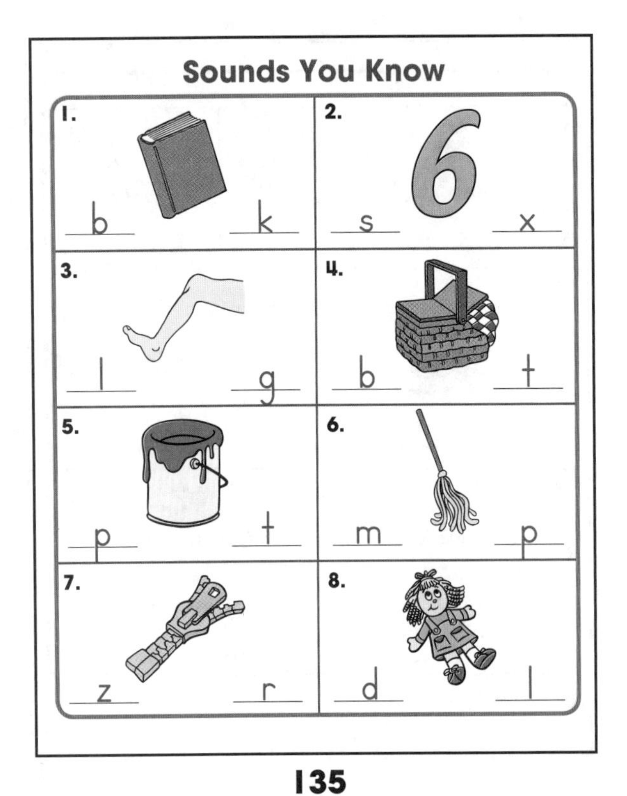
Sounds You Know

1. b k
2. s x
3. l g
4. b t
5. p t
6. m p
7. z r
8. d l

135

Notes

Notes

Notes